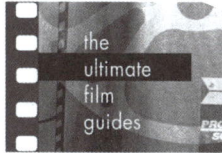

the
ultimate
film
guides

Seven Samurai (Shichinin no samurai)

Director
Akira Kurosawa

Note by Roy Stafford

Longman   York Press

Japanese transliterations follow the most recent work on Kurosawa from
Mitsuhiro Yoshimoto, so the samurai leader is Kanbei rather than Kambei
etc.

York Press
322 Old Brompton Road, London SW5 9JH

Pearson Education Limited
Edinburgh Gate, Harlow, Essex CM20 2JE, United Kingdom
Associated companies, branches and representatives throughout
the world

First published 2001

ISBN 0-582-45256-2

Designed by Vicki Pacey
Illustrations by Brett Breckon
Phototypeset by Land & Unwin (Data Sciences) Northampton
Printed in Malaysia, KVP

contents

Cinema resembles so many other arts. If cinema has very literary characteristics, it also has theatrical qualities, a philosophical side, attributes of painting and sculpture and musical elements. But cinema is, in the final analysis, cinema.

Akira Kurosawa (1975), translated by Audie E. Bock

author of this note   Roy Stafford is a freelance lecturer and writer working in film education in the North of England. This is his second York Film Note, following *La Haine* in 2000.

background

trailer

Director Akira Kurosawa has given this a virile mounting... High adventure and excitement are stamped all over this solid-core film.

Variety 8 September 1954, from Venice Film Festival

Kurosawa's *Seven Samurai* (1954) is as riveting today as it was when it was released, an annihilating melodrama that works equally well on the epic and the intimate scale.

Gary Morris, Bright Lights Film Journal, *September 1996, issue 17*

...that masterpiece of carnage and courage... *Seven Samurai*: the best of all battle epics... with its just war, hopeless odds, camaraderie of soldiers, and final, lonely fate of the outsider/warrior.

Michael Wilmington, Film Comment, *January 1999, vol 35, no 1*

While the casual viewer will appreciate the film's visual style and dramatic power without necessarily being aware of the technical mastery involved, the film maker and film student will find in *Seven Samurai* an impressive deployment of the full arsenal of cinematic techniques at the service of the narrative.

Gary Crowdus, Cinéaste *1993, vol XIX no 4*

The Internet Movie Database (IMDb) carries a list of the 'Top 250' movies of all time, based on the votes cast by its 'users'. In 2001, the Number 9 film on the list was a Japanese film made in black and white in 1954. Set in the sixteenth century and running over 200 minutes, *Shichinin no samurai*

brilliance of Kurosawa's filming and editing

(*Seven Samurai*) is at first sight an unusual selection for a 'popular' list of top films. What explains its status?

In the history of cinema there are very few films that can be seen in retrospect to have marked a change in the use of film techniques and the conception of what cinema can achieve. Such films have influenced succeeding generations of film makers and yet they remain undiminished by time and attempts at imitation: *Battleship Potemkin*, *Citizen Kane*, *Roma città aperta*, *A bout de souffle* are some such films. *Seven Samurai* belongs in this select category, and its director Akira Kurosawa belongs with **Eisenstein**, Welles, Rossellini and Godard as a major figure in the history of cinema, whose films are essential viewing.

There are many reasons for the importance of *Seven Samurai*. Its appearance at the Venice Film Festival in 1954 confirmed the quality of Japanese Cinema for international critics and similarly confirmed the stature of its director and its star (Toshiro Mifune), suggested by the earlier appearance of *Rashomon* in 1950. Although set firmly in the past, the film also helped to re-introduce Japan to the west after the terrible humiliation of the postwar American Occupation (1945–52). The combination of exciting action and a strong story, of 'humanism' and 'heroism', provided the model for much of the action cinema that followed in the 1960s, and the brilliance of Kurosawa's filming and editing techniques impressed film makers across the world, but especially in Hollywood.

John Sturges 'remade' *Seven Samurai* as *The Magnificent Seven* in 1960, but the film that most strikingly employs Kurosawa's techniques is Sam Peckinpah's *The Wild Bunch* made in 1969 ('I want to make Westerns like Kurosawa makes Westerns', Peckinpah said). Later in his career, when out of favour in Japan, Kurosawa benefited from the support of fans amongst the so-called 'movie brat' generation of George Lucas and Francis Ford Coppola.

In Japan, Kurosawa was a controversial figure, often at odds with the **studio system** and especially with the critics. He found an appreciative popular audience and by the early 1960s his revision of traditional genre formats dominated the Japanese box office. Yet many critics attacked him for making films for the international market. They called him the 'most

American' of Japanese directors and argued that his films were successful in the west because of their 'exoticism'. It is difficult to fathom why this view developed. Kurosawa himself remained above such criticism, but his dignity was sometimes taken to be arrogance. His nickname was 'sensei' – the master, or 'the Emperor' – an ironic title for a devout antimilitarist and humanist. His mastery came from complete devotion to making films and close attention to detail – perfectionism perhaps.

For audiences in the west, Kurosawa has been the best known director in Japanese cinema. For film scholars, he has usually been bracketed with two of his contemporaries in the 1950s – Kenji Mizoguchi and Yasujiro Ozu. Of the two, Mizoguchi came to the attention of western critics at the same time as Kurosawa and provided a useful contrast, especially with his period films, made in a very different style. Ozu waited longer for recognition in the west, but with Mizoguchi vied for the title of 'most Japanese' director in Japan. Ozu's static camera and Mizoguchi's elegant tracking shots are quite distinct from the bravura camerawork of *Seven Samurai*.

It is the vitality of the imagery, the audacity of the editing, the subtle use of sound and the quality of the acting performances that audiences remember from *Seven Samurai*. Most of all, over the 200 minutes, there is an astonishing range of cinematography – with long shots and 'big close-ups' reminiscent of Eisenstein, **'deep focus'** interiors and painterly compositions of landscapes, **tracking shots** and swift **wipes**, high and low angles and **jump cuts**. *Seven Samurai* is like a 'how to' manual of cinematic techniques.

reading seven samurai

In sixteenth-century Japan a small village is regularly raided by a large band of brigands who carry off the harvest and sometimes the women of the community. In desperation the villagers hire a disparate group of seven 'masterless' samurai – professional warriors – who organise the defence of the village, helping the farmers to defeat the brigands. The next harvest is planted and life goes on.

In bald outline a formulaic action film, under Kurosawa's direction *Seven Samurai* becomes a story of courage and co-operation in the context of a

exhilarating as action, fascinating as visual spectacle

realistic struggle to survive in a harsh economic and social environment. The farmers and the samurai are not natural allies and in other circumstances could be at each other's throats. There are no moral certainties and the faceless bandits who threaten the village could once have been farmers or even rogue samurai. In an intensely 'human' story Kurosawa presents two powerful characterisations: Kanbei, as the ultimate professional man of honour who organises the defence, and Kikuchiyo, the catalyst of the narrative, the orphan farmer's son who strives to be a samurai (in comic and tragic fashion) and in doing so draws the audience into the complexities of relationships between social classes in the sixteenth century, but also into the quandaries facing Japan in the 1950s.

Kurosawa's triumph is to pull the audience on to the edges of their seats in anticipation of the next sequence of action and to intrigue them with a myriad of secondary themes that explore the contrasting lives of farmers and samurai. The film is exhilarating as action, fascinating as visual spectacle and ultimately satisfying as human drama.

key players' biographies

AKIRA KUROSAWA

Kurosawa (1910–98) was born in Tokyo, the seventh child of a man of samurai stock who became a teacher in military school. The family was lower middle class and, at this time, reasonably prosperous. Kurosawa did not follow his father, either in athletic prowess or a yearning for military life. He was not academically gifted but his interest in art and history prospered under a number of progressive teachers who stood out amongst the conventional background of primary and middle schools. Kendo, the traditional Japanese fencing art, and calligraphy were the only two of his father's passions he took up. But his father did take him to the cinema, especially to American and European films in the second half of the Taisho period (1912–26).

Kurosawa moved on to a school of western painting when he was eighteen and then struggled to make a living as a commercial artist at a time when his family were beginning to suffer economic hardship. He joined the Japan Proletariat Artists' Group and became immersed in Russian literature. With an elder brother working as a **benshi** (a narrator-commentator in silent films) in a Tokyo cinema, it was perhaps inevitable that Kurosawa would eventually try to enter the film industry. In 1936 he answered a newspaper advertisement and won a competition to become a scriptwriter for the small company that soon became the major studio, Toho. He wrote many screenplays while working as an assistant director and gained confidence when he joined the team led by director Kajiro Yamamoto.

Akira Kurosawa's first directing opportunity came during the Second World War and *Sanshiro Sugata* in 1943 told the story of a judo student who fights in order to discover himself. Working under the watchful eye of the military censors must have been very difficult for Kurosawa, radical and antimilitary since his schooldays. After the war, he quickly became one of the leading directors of the 'new generation' although he was still working under censorship conditions – this time controlled by the American authorities.

Rashomon (1950), *Hakuchi* (1951), an adaptation of Dostoevsky's *The Idiot*, *Ikiru* (1952), a moving drama about a business man dying of cancer, and *Seven Samurai* launched Kurosawa's 'golden period'. The films that followed were successful internationally (e.g. his acclaimed adaptation of *Macbeth* as *Throne of Blood* (1957) and *The Hidden Fortress* (1958), a point of inspiration for George Lucas in the making of *Star Wars* (US 1977)). The two samurai films, again starring Toshiro Mifune, *Yojimbo* (1961) and *Sanjuro* (1962) were also big hits in Japan. The 'golden period' lasted until the mid 1960s and *Red Beard* (1965). At this point he made the mistake of becoming involved with a Hollywood studio in the making of *Tora! Tora!*, the epic film about the Japanese attack on Pearl Harbour. Kurosawa found it impossible to work in the Hollywood environment (or perhaps Twentieth Century Fox found it impossible to work with Kurosawa – either way he withdrew from the production).

It took several years to put together his next film, *Dodeskaden* in 1970, and in his later career, Kurosawa lost support from commercial funders in Japan

Toshiro Mifune and Akira Kurosawa
(right) during a break in the
shooting of *Yojimbo*

seen to communicate universal human values

and struggled to make more 'personal' films, mostly with foreign backing. Although many critics saw these later films as lesser achievements than those of the 1950s, they were still outstanding in terms of world cinema and the highlights such as *Kagemusha* (1980) and *Ran* (1985) once again inspired young film makers. The last films made by Kurosawa in the 1990s have not been widely seen in the west, but they continued to be rated highly by the specialist film magazine *Kinema jumpo* in Japan. In the later period of his career, Japanese critics perhaps began to reasses Kurosawa as a 'film artist' – he had, after all, survived the demise of the powerful **studio system** in Japan and carried on making films. When Kurosawa died in 1998 the flood of tributes from critics, fans and film makers alike confirmed his status as a major film artist.

Given the 'most western of Japanese directors' tag, it is ironic that the Kurosawa films most widely seen in the west are primarily historical and present a feudal and alien culture to European and American audiences. It is Kurosawa's approach to his subjects that makes the films accessible and aligns them with other classics of the 1950s' humanist art cinema from directors like Satyajit Ray and Jean Renoir, both Kurosawa admirers, who were seen to communicate universal human values rather than 'alien' cultures. Kurosawa also made contemporary films and worked for many years within the confines of the distinctive Japanese studio system and it is unfortunate that these films do not have the same high profile in international film history. (A full filmography is given at the end of this book and Kurosawa's work in the 1940s is contextualised in Context.)

TOSHIRO MIFUNE

More than any other actor, Toshiro Mifune (1920–97) is associated with the films of Akira Kurosawa. He starred in ten consecutive Kurosawa films, from *Seven Samurai* (1954) to *Red Beard* (1965), and sixteen in all. He was born and raised in the Japanese colony of Manchuria and served in the Imperial Air Force during the Second World War. Mifune had never been to Japan before he applied for a job at Toho studios in 1945. According to Owen (1984) he turned up for an interview as a camera operator, but by mistake was asked to audition as an actor. Irritated by the mistake he put on a show of aggression and bluster that intrigued Kurosawa.

Mifune had extraordinary screen presence

> Mifune had a kind of talent I had never encountered before in the Japanese film world. It was, above all, the speed with which he expressed himself that was astounding. The ordinary Japanese actor might need ten feet of film to get across an impression; Mifune needed only three. The speed of his movements was such that he said in a single action what took ordinary actors three separate movements to express. He put forth everything directly and boldly, and his sense of timing was the keenest I had ever seen in a Japanese actor. And yet with all his quickness, he also had surprisingly fine sensibilities.
>
> *Kurosawa, 1983, p. 161*

Mifune became established quickly and was already starring for Kurosawa by 1948. His was the presence that astounded western audiences in *Rashomon*, the film that introduced Kurosawa and Japanese Cinema to the rest of the world in 1950. Mifune had extraordinary screen presence and it is significant that although he is not the 'leader' of the samurai in *Seven Samurai*, he is still the central focus of the narrative. Mifune became the most recognisable Japanese face in cinema for the international audience and eventually found his way to Hollywood. Perhaps the best of his Hollywood work was in *Hell in the Pacific*, the two-hander directed by John Boorman in 1968, in which he and Lee Marvin are two isolated Second World War combatants. His iconic status appeared to be confirmed in 1999 when the third official 'Dogme' film from Denmark was entitled *Mifune* and featured a character who liked to dress up as Kikuchiyo in *Seven Samurai*.

TAKASHI SHIMURA

Shimura (1905–82) who plays Kanbei, the leader of the samurai, was even more of a Kurosawa regular than Mifune. More of a character actor and less of a flamboyant star, he typified the values of Kurosawa's cinema in twenty films, from *Sanshiro Sugata* in 1943 to *Kagemusha* in 1980. There is a temptation amongst western film scholars to think of Shimura as the 'Ward Bond' to Mifune's 'John Wayne' when comparing Kurosawa's films with those of **John Ford**. Shimura has something of Bond's solidity and authority, as well as a physical resemblance, but he was an actor of greater range and with an intelligence and gentleness that is so apparent in *Seven Samurai*.

director as auteur

Akira Kurosawa was a 'film artist', a director of 'personal films'. With his reputation established in the west by the 1960s, he was elevated to the position of film 'author' or auteur. However, this description is slightly confusing because it masks the very different circumstances under which Kurosawa worked, compared to the Hollywood and European directors similarly championed at this time and still given a form of privileged status in contemporary film criticism.

The term auteur gradually gained currency in the 1950s just as Kurosawa's films began to be released in the west. There had been the acceptance of certain film makers as 'film artists' since the 1920s. **Sergei Eisenstein** and Fritz Lang were just two of the European directors whose work in the 1920s was so distinctive that it attracted attention in film clubs and societies across the world. American directors such as Charles Chaplin and John Ford also attracted attention between the 1920s and 1950s because they seemed able to maintain some control over their work despite having to deal with Hollywood studios. But in the early 1950s, young critics working on French film magazines like *Cahiers du cinéma* and *Positif* began to develop the idea of film authorship. They turned it into a polemic against one sort of cinema and in favour of another. The 'manifesto' of this critics' group was a famous essay by François Truffaut published in 1954 as 'Une certaine tendance du cinéma'. Truffaut's target was the concept of 'quality cinema' – the studio-bound commercial cinema with highly polished scripts, trained actors, expensive sets and conventional stories, often based on literary or theatrical adaptations.

Truffaut wanted to see something very different – a new cinema in which the director was king and in which the techniques of cinema, largely subsumed under the concept of mise-en-scène, could be used to express the director's personal vision (of the world and of cinema). The critical writing of Truffaut and his colleagues coalesced into *la politique des auteurs* which was mistranslated by the American critic Andrew Sarris to become

director as auteur background

searching to express a personal vision

'auteur theory'. It was not a theory but a polemic – an argument that there should be films made by directors seeking to express themselves, rather than just 'telling stories'. The subsequent writing on the idea of authorship strove to identify both personal 'style' in the application of cinematic techniques and a personal 'thematic'. This was sometimes taken to the extreme by the suggestion that each auteur had a single grand project, endlessly making the same film, and searching to express a personal vision as effectively as possible.

Through their critical writing, Truffaut and colleagues like Jean-Luc Godard, Claude Chabrol, Eric Rohmer and Jacques Rivette (all of whom would become auteurs themselves as part of the **French New Wave** at the end of the decade) promoted the surviving 'artists' of pre-1939 cinema, the new group of Italian **neo-realists** and those Hollywood directors whose films showed 'personal expression' despite working under the restrictions of the Hollywood studio system.

Akira Kurosawa and Kenji Mizoguchi came to the attention of western critics in the early 1950s. It was clear that these were 'master' film makers capable of utilising a wide range of cinematic techniques. After the release of one or two films it was also clear that their films showed thematic continuities and a distinctive 'personal vision'. *Seven Samurai* found Kurosawa at the point in his career when he was able to move out of the studio lot and challenge the conventions of genre film making. Up to this point Kurosawa had worked both within the Japanese studio system for Toho and in a quasi-independent way when the Communist-led film trade unions in Japan took industrial action against Toho in the late 1940s. This forced Kurosawa into short-term arrangements with other studios. He returned to Toho in 1952 and gradually established a new relationship with the studio, which, by the 1960s, saw his films listed as 'Toho/ Kurosawa productions'. Kurosawa worked within an industrial film industry that in the 1950s produced more films than any other in the world. At the same time, audiences in the west saw Kurosawa's work alongside that of Satyajit Ray, the Bengali film maker working completely outside the Indian film industry. The work of both directors was accommodated within the broad category of 'Art Cinema' from the 1950s through to the mid 1970s, i.e. through the period of the high point of 'auteur cinema'.

'auteurism' ... began to lose favour

Contrary to this view of art cinema production is the 'collective' endeavour of Kurosawa and his consistent collaborators – not just his 'stock company' of actors and stars like Mifune and Shimura, but also writers, composers, cinematographers, set designers and numerous others. In this sense Kurosawa can be bracketed with Ford, Hitchcock, Hawks etc. as major director/producers who worked with studios on a 'special relationship' basis. This reference to collaboration leads into another area of auteurist critical work – the attempt to explain a director's work via a study of his (rarely 'her') personal life. Kurosawa devoted his life to cinema, beginning as an assistant director to Kajiro Yamamoto – 'Yama-san'. As Philip Kemp (1999) points out, although Yamamoto was generally regarded as a director of 'lightweight' films, he was an acknowledged master technician. He was also a relatively young man and an excellent teacher. Kurosawa is unstinting of his praise for his mentor and often referred to his apprenticeship and how much he learned about every aspect of film making. Kurosawa believed that a director should know about every other role. This meant that he could work closely with every member of his team and particularly with his editor. The experience of the teacher-student relationship was so important to Kurosawa that it featured in several of his films and is evident in *Seven Samurai* in Katsushiro's plea to become Kanbei's pupil. It reappears as the central relationship in *Red Beard* (1965). Kurosawa himself became the *sensei* – the master for his own younger crew and actors.

From the 1970s onwards, 'auteurism' as an approach within academic film studies began to lose favour and was replaced by an interest in genre studies and other approaches focusing on national and personal identities. However, the concept of the 'film author' remained in more general writing on film and in particular as a means of promoting films and as a focus for publishing. In the latest academic publication on Kurosawa and his films, *Kurosawa: Film Studies and Japanese Cinema* by Mitsuhiro Yoshimoto (2000), the author 'does what it says on the cover' – he tries to relate a study of Kurosawa's films to the context of both developments within film studies and critical practice and within Japanese culture generally:

director as auteur background

'complexity, contradiction, and openness'

> ...this study is neither an example of auteur criticism nor a subspecies of national cinema studies. Kurosawa is not an auteur who single-mindedly pursued throughout his career, which spanned more than fifty years, a single project, whether artistic, political or otherwise. Nor is he a representative Japanese film maker who, despite his interests in Western art, literature and film, relied on traditional Japanese aesthetics and sensibility as a foundation for his films' style and worldview. For Kurosawa, 'Japan' is not an answer but a problem to be scrutinised. Nothing in his films gives us any privileged access to Japanese aesthetics, sensibility, cultural heritage, or Japaneseness. The complexity, contradiction, and openness of Kurosawa's work cannot be reduced to either the intention and subjectivity of an auteur or the cultural traditions and patterns of a particular nation called Japan.
>
> *Yoshimoto, 2000, p 375–6*

Yoshimoto's aim is shared by this Note which attempts to present *Seven Samurai* as a collaboration between Akira Kurosawa and his actors and creative team in the context of both Japanese and international cinema in 1954.

narrative & form

The idea behind *Seven Samurai* is deceptively simple – a group of farmers, threatened by the attack of a large group of merciless bandits who steal their harvest every year, decide to hire samurai to defend their village. This could almost be the basis for a modern '**High Concept**' Hollywood movie in which the narrative idea can be expressed in twenty-five words or less. Arguably, *The Magnificent Seven*, the Hollywood remake of *Seven Samurai*, is indeed a relatively straightforward playing out of this simple idea. Yet in the hands of Akira Kurosawa, *Seven Samurai* becomes a much more complex narrative, more than justifying its long running time.

> *Seven Samurai* is not an adventure film from my point of view. It's about the relationship of the samurai and the farmers and I wanted to describe the character of each samurai.
>
> *Kurosawa, 1986*

So, although it includes some of the finest action scenes ever filmed, *Seven Samurai* also finds time for complex emotional drama and psychological exploration of character. The 'familiarity' of the action sequences and the behaviour of the samurai that derives to some extent from western audiences' knowledge of Hollywood action genres, masks the more complex play of forces in a Japanese context, where questions of class or caste are crucially important. In an American context, the film would appear to be about the 'success' of the samurai in defeating the bandits. But the final moment of *Seven Samurai* has Kanbei, the samurai leader, observing the villagers' energy and high spirits in planting a new crop and remarking: 'We've lost, yet again'; 'With their land, it's the farmers who are the victors ... not us.'

genre in japanese & american cinema

In Contexts, there is some discussion of the Japanese film industry and traditional Japanese approaches to narrative. Here we should simply note that *Seven Samurai* (like most of Kurosawa's work and that of the veteran Kenji Mizoguchi at this time) was directly opposed to the popular historical genres of the time. The ***chanbara*** or swordplay genre tended to be set in the more stable **Tokugawa or Edo** period (1600–1868) when 'clean-cut' individual samurai would engage each other in ritualised contests, with nothing at stake except their own skins. Such films were perhaps similar to routine 'gunplay' Hollywood Westerns or 'swashbucklers'. Nobody had previously made a film in which villagers hired samurai or which had the same concern with class difference.

If *Seven Samurai* was revolutionary in a Japanese context, it perhaps looked more familiar to audiences in the west. The film uses many of the elements of the 'combat picture' – a subgenre of the war film that dates back at least as far as **John Ford's** *The Lost Patrol* in 1934 and which flourished in British and American Cinema during and after the Second World War. The basic idea involves the selection of a small group of men for a specific combat mission. The group will comprise men from different backgrounds (in Britain signified by class and regional accents), each with some kind of identifying personal characteristic – physical appearance, attitude, personality trait etc. – and each will probably have some form of personal adventure during the film. The idea has persisted beyond the strictly military story to encompass 'action adventure films' such as *The Dirty Dozen*, *Kelly's Heroes* and more recently, *Three Kings*. With the exception of *Three Kings*, most of these films do not have the extra dimension of *Seven Samurai* in offering 'action' in the context of a realist depiction of an historical period and extending the narrative beyond the combat group to include the local community (and, as argued below, to make the community the driving force of the narrative). Nevertheless, the 'selection process' adopted to form the samurai group and the ensuing adventures would be familiar genre devices for western audiences.

A second obvious (American) generic reference is to the 'Western', or at least to one specific (arguably the single most important) creator of Westerns, John Ford. Much has been written about Kurosawa's admiration for Ford and it sometimes feels as if the comparison between the two serves to diminish the Japanese director's achievements at the expense of the American – as if Kurosawa is somehow copying Ford. This is an unworthy notion and should be pushed firmly aside, but it is impossible for any film viewer brought up on a steady diet of the stream of classic Westerns and other genre pictures made by Ford over a fifty-year career not to recognise some of the same images and narrative devices at work in *Seven Samurai*. Ford himself must have been aware of this and may well have been amused by his own decision to make *Seven Women* in 1960 (missionaries held captive by a Chinese warlord).

Ford was famous for a number of Westerns that are concerned primarily with the 'taming of the west', the building of communities and the development of law and good government – in other words, Westerns focusing on American social history rather than 'gunplay'. In many ways, the Seventh Cavalry was Ford's idea of a community in the desert of the American southwest. His 'cavalry trilogy' of *Fort Apache*, *She Wore a Yellow Ribbon* and *Rio Grande* were made in the late 1940s and these films, along with *Wagonmaster* (1950), another 'community-based' narrative, would have been available to Kurosawa around the early 1950s. These films explore the role of the individual within the group, a theme recognisable in the story of Wyatt Earp and the building of the township in *My Darling Clementine* (1946) and in the dilemmas facing the central character of John Wayne's cavalry officer in the trilogy. There is certainly a strong similarity between the samurai and the cavalry troop in terms of identifiable individuals who must sacrifice something for the good of the community. (However, there are also distinct differences between the rather 'idealised' communities of Ford's films and the more 'human' and 'realist' communities of Kurosawa.)

The theme of the individual and the group is central to Kurosawa's work and perhaps he did borrow some narrative ideas from American models. But he translated these models into something distinctively Japanese and the comparisons that have been made between *Seven Samurai* and

Hollywood (see Anderson, 1962 and Parshall, 1989) tend to validate Kurosawa at the expense of Hollywood – interestingly, there are no prominent critical comparisons directly with Ford.

narrative structure

The most universally applicable approach to narrative is that associated with the work of **Tzvetan Todorov**. He suggests that narratives begin with a period of equilibrium – a balance of conflicting forces. This is disrupted to create a dramatic conflict, the climax of which enables the establishment of a new equilibrium, slightly different from the former balance.

In Hollywood this model is apparent in the designation of the so-called 'three act' structure that requires an opening exposition of the problem, a second act of escalating conflict reaching a climax and a short third act which allows 'resolution' of the problem – usually expressed in Hollywood as a 'happy ending'. Kurosawa himself refers to the structure of a screenplay as being like that of a symphony in three or four movements with different tempos. He also suggests in his comments to would-be Japanese film makers that, 'one can use the **Noh** play with its three-part structure: *jo* (introduction), *ha* (destruction) and *kyu* (haste). If you devote yourself fully to Noh and gain something good from this, it will emerge naturally in your films. ...But in a screenplay, I think the symphonic structure is the easiest for the people of today to understand' (Kurosawa, 1983, p. 193). Noh theatre is discussed briefly in Contexts.

Seven Samurai is twice the length of the standard Hollywood feature and Kurosawa uses the extra screen time to open out the 'symphonic' structure into several distinct sections:

■ the opening, in which the threat of the bandit attack and the problems of the farmers are set out

■ the farmers' decision to hire samurai, their trip to the town and initial failure to find samurai

■ the appearance of Kanbei and the introduction of the seven samurai

■ the samurai journey to the village and the preparations for battle

intensely human stories

- the escalating conflict with the bandits, culminating in the 'final battle'
- the closing sequence in which the farmers begin their planting of the rice crop and the surviving samurai mourn their dead colleagues

No doubt some of these separate sections could be combined in order to represent the narrative in three or four 'movements', but breaking it down in this way helps to foreground Kurosawa's concern to make the conflict a matter of different value systems, representing what he saw as the 'reality' of sixteenth-century Japan and, by extension, modern Japan. The farmers mistrust the samurai and both realise that without their identity in the system they could be forced to join the bandits (who, in their own way are also a 'community', but one based on no other principle than survival and desire). At the end of the film the farmers virtually ignore the samurai, gaining strength in their celebration of the timeless planting ritual.

Is this a 'happy ending'? Kurosawa suggests that the samurai have been engaged in a more or less hopeless quest. They have gained nothing from it, except perhaps a confirmation of their sense of honour. As the planting ritual suggests, farming will continue no matter what. The system has not been changed – new bandits will appear, the farmers will still hide their harvests and no doubt will still murder samurai and steal their armour.

While this analysis of the brutal medieval society is compelling, Kurosawa also offers us intensely human stories and examples of individual bravery and compassion. As in many film narratives, it is the validity of these representations that is remembered rather than the narrative resolution. The creation and treatment of the characters is therefore crucially important.

character

Seven Samurai has a large cast forty bandits, as many or more villagers and the samurai themselves, not to mention the townspeople and travellers. Most have only minor roles as figures in the 'landscape of battle' or other crowd scenes. But an unusually large number are associated with the main narrative elements of the film. They are created mainly as 'types' (but see

character

we understand their motivation

below) – we recognise them as having a particular role in the community or as being representative of a particular human quality, perhaps conveyed through physical appearance or acting style. A point should be made here about casting – the villagers who are named and all the samurai characters are quite distinctive in appearance. This has the great advantage of aiding the spectator in following the story, but also helps to create the impression of more 'rounded' characters. If they are comic or grotesque, they are also given sufficient individuality to allow us to perceive the humanity of their situation – we understand their motivation.

Very few of the characters, even the samurai, are given a **'back story'** – an explanation of what has happened in the past and how they come to be in the situation in which they find themselves. The exceptions are Kikuchiyo, played by Toshiro Mifune, and Rikichi, the young village man who in the opening sequence seems keenest to fight the bandits.

KIKUCHIYO

Toshiro Mifune was to some extent Kurosawa's prodigy and he had become a star in Kurosawa's 1948 film *Drunken Angel*. He then appeared as the lead in many of Kurosawa's later films. Although Takashi Shimura as Kanbei heads the cast list (he was a major star and had led Kurosawa's *Ikiru* in 1952), the opening titles announce Mifune as playing Kikuchiyo. No other actor is given this prominence and it is reasonable to assume that Kurosawa will in some way 'speak' through the character of Kikuchiyo.

Mifune plays the role in a very 'over the top' manner and if the character is in some way Kurosawa's 'representative', it seems initially to be a strange choice. Kikuchiyo first appears as a clown with a desperate wish to be accepted as a samurai. His ambition is not helped by his loutish behaviour, and Kanbei, otherwise a courteous man, dismisses him without hesitation. Yet as the narrative progresses it is Kikuchiyo who invariably brings 'reality' to bear, albeit unconsciously on occasions. He seems to understand in his buffoonish way how and why the farmers behave and what to do to persuade them, so when the samurai arrive in the village only to find it deserted, it is Kikuchiyo who flushes the farmers out by sounding the alarm.

Gradually his 'back story' emerges, to be confirmed in the incident when he carries the baby from the burning mill. 'This is me!' he cries, explaining how he was a baby orphaned by bandits. His relationships with the children in the village are a central feature of the construction of his character.

Kikuchiyo was a farmer's son. He wants to become a samurai, but he could easily have become a bandit. He is not a noble or heroic figure, although he dies a noble death, avenging the swordsman Kyuzo. Yet he is the agent in the narrative through whom 'reality' is introduced into the action story. This is Kurosawa's aim and it is best illustrated by the moment when Kikuchiyo appears in the centre of the village with the collection of samurai armour. At first he doesn't realise why Kanbei looks so stony-faced and it takes a few moments for us to realise that these seemingly helpless farmers have previously either murdered lone samurai or robbed the corpses of samurai who have fallen in battle. Kikuchiyo then turns on both the farmers and the samurai – because it is the samurai who through their harsh treatment of farmers in the past have turned them into murderers and thieves. At the end of his tirade, Kikuchiyo leaves the samurai sleeping house and moves in with Rikichi in a stable. Even then he has to urge Rikichi to stay in the stable, scolding him for giving up his house to the samurai. (Kikuchiyo is also the one who first uncovers the evidence of Rikichi's wife, although he doesn't know it.) The caste divisions and their observance by both farmers and samurai are brought to prominence in this sequence.

If the main theme of the film is the submission of the individual to the collective – without losing the qualities which make individuals unique – it is through the learning process, that Kikuchiyo experiences, that we learn as an audience. Peter Parshall presents an excellent analysis of this process (Parshall, 1989). Although he is the star, Mifune must share the action sequences with the other actors. But he is often 'privileged': the camera picks him out. Kanbei might be expected to be the focus of attention because he expresses Kurosawa's humanistic vision. As Parshall argues.

> Ideal characters make for dull films, however, and Kurosawa wisely focuses more on Kikuchiyo. Although the action of the film

> concerns the samurai saving the village, the psychological center
> of the film is the re-education of Kikuchiyo.
>
> *Parshall, p. 277*

Kikuchiyo begins as the 'outside' figure on the banner that Heihachi creates for the struggle. There are six circles representing the samurai, the *ta* character signifying the village and a triangle for Kikuchiyo. But when he dies, killing the bandit leader in the last act of the battle, the camera privileges his death, holding a long shot of his fallen body and, when a cut reveals Kanbei and the others, they are beneath the fallen Kikuchiyo who is lying on a platform. In death he joins the group, being buried in samurai style with his sword in the funeral mound alongside Kuzeo, Heihachi and Gorobei. The selfish, individualistic Kikuchiyo of the opening scenes does not lose his individuality and his distinctive personality, but he absorbs and internalises the samurai values of sacrifice for the group.

RIKICHI & HIS WIFE

Rikichi is the first of the farmers to suggest fighting the bandits. No explanation is given as to why he is so vehement about fighting and at first we assume that it is simply his youth. Significantly he breaks away from the group when his idea is rejected. But later he is given a close-up and the camera lingers on his face as he asks Manzo what he will give to the bandits to appease them – his pretty daughter Shinto perhaps? This is during the last sequence before the appearance of Kanbei and the salvation of the farmers.

This lingering moment is recalled during the raid on the bandits' fort. Rikichi leads Kyuzo, Kukichiyo and Heihachi to the hideout and sets fire to the building, taking a full part in the slaughter that follows. As the samurai peer through openings in the wall of the fort, the camera picks out a beautiful young woman who rises from her sleep but does nothing when she sees the smoke and to the samurai's amazement does not betray them. For a short while the camera lingers on the woman in medium close-up as a Noh flute plays on the soundtrack. This strange interlude appears meaningless at the time, but it does recall the earlier shot of Rikichi.

Moments later when the killing stops and the samurai retreat across the river, Rikichi goes back to confront the woman who has wandered out from the building. She screams in horror when she sees Rikichi and runs back into the flames. Rikichi tries to follow her but is repelled by the heat. Heihachi rushes to him to drag him away and is shot. In despair, Rikichi helps the other two samurai carry the dying Heihachi away. When they reach safety Kukichiyo berates Rikichi who shouts that the woman was his wife and prostrates himself as Heihachi finally lurches to his death.

This little scene encapsulates many of the themes of the film. Rikichi is by far the most courageous and intelligent of the villagers and the most capable of fighting like a samurai. But the events reveal him to be motivated by revenge for the loss of his wife whom he clearly loved (and who loved him so much that she could not face him after her defilement by the bandits). This could be a more acceptable human motivation than the greed shown by other farmers. Yet it is an individual motivation, unlike the collective decisions of the village and the code of the samurai, and, because of it, the 'innocent' Heihachi is killed. This is reality – Rikichi's love for his wife leads to an innocent death. This is further emphasised by the selection of Heihachi as the samurai who dies. When he is introduced Gorobei says that he is only an average warrior when it comes to fighting, but that his good humour will help to cheer everyone up. So Heihachi offered a talent that all could share and he has been lost because of Rikichi's selfish desire for revenge.

THE SAMURAI

Apart from Kukichiyo, the samurai are mysterious figures without history. Kanbei is a natural leader admired and respected by everybody. Where has he come from, how has he gained this stature? All we know is that he is a *ronin* – a masterless samurai. Perhaps he was a leader in the army of a lord who was defeated? He is the perfect leader who knows when to discipline his troops (e.g. his treatment of Kikuchiyo and of the wavering villagers) and when to allow them to be individuals (Kuzeo is allowed to go off and capture a gun, but Kikuchiyo is criticised for the same action – Kanbei knows Kuzeo can be trusted as a 'professional'). He is confident of his own fighting abilities, but not prepared to risk lives without good reason. All this flows from his first appearance when he is prepared to have his head shaved (a shaming act for a samurai) in order to catch a thief – an act he performs for no obvious reward.

Above, reference is made to Kikuchiyo as Kurosawa's 'voice' in the film, but Anderson (1962) argues that it is Kanbei who represents Kurosawa as an autobiographical figure. In other words, Kurosawa selects Kikuchiyo as the driving force of the narrative, but Kanbei, like the director, is the narrator of the story. He would also be the 'controller' of the story, except that Kurosawa suggests that the story can't be controlled – this is how people are and how they will act. There is an argument here as to whether the narrative centre is Kikuchiyo's re-education or Kanbei's final discovery of 'reality' (see below).

The other samurai all represent the positive qualities of the elite group. Gorobei accepts the job because he is fascinated by Kanbei's character that matches his own wit and intellect, Shichiroji joins up with his old friend through loyalty, Heihachi is phlegmatic and good-natured. Kuzeo is the almost silent swordsman, introduced as the victor of a duel he has been forced to fight and later granted a moment of tranquillity amongst the flowers. Richie (1996) suggests that the floral scene confirms his status in the film as representative of the Japanese warrior spirit, **Bushido**.

Katsushiro is a familiar type from western cinema – the young man who reveres his elders (as befits a young would-be samurai) and is keen to fight, but is distracted by a first romance. Kurosawa has him endlessly referred to as a child and emphasises his lack of 'manly' samurai qualities by casting a young actor who is supremely 'good-looking' rather than ruggedly handsome. Katsushiro is just one of a series of characters in *Seven Samurai* who might be found in a John Ford film of the late 1940s, like the young officers courting the commander's niece in *Fort Apache*.

Katsushiro is given no back story, but he plays a crucial role in both the romance and in emphasising the seriousness of killing. When he finally kills a bandit in the final battle, he falls to his knees with a mixture of horror and relief. The romance is important because, like the revelations about Kikuchiyo, it points to the caste division between samurai and farmers. The young couple are in love, but they know that their marriage would be unacceptable – again this is emphasised by the selection of the samurai who watch them in the rain. It is Kuzeo, least likely to speak about what he has seen (because he rarely speaks anyway) but also the most pure embodiment of the warrior spirit (he also 'shares' the flowers with the lovers). At the end of the film Katsushiro looks wistfully at Shino, but after a slight hesitation, she goes off to join the others in planting the new rice crop.

THE VILLAGERS

Several villagers are picked out and named because they have a specific role to play. Manzo is the father of Shino and represents the worst aspects of the devious farmer mentality – hiding his wealth and bartering for his freedom. Shino herself is given little to do apart from attracting Katsushiro and then rejecting him at the end of the film when she sees that her future lies with the village.

Yohei is presented as a figure of fun – he appears at the beginning of the film like a startled rabbit, overhearing the bandits' plans, and later he wears the samurai armour in a comical attempt to act like a warrior. It is Yohei's horse that Kikuchiyo attempts to ride in another of the film's comic sequences. But in the scenes in the town, Yohei is mocked by the ruffians in the boarding house, and here he becomes a sympathetic character who cries at the thought of his wife's suffering if the bandits return. Yohei dies in Kikuchiyo's arms, gasping that he did his best to look out for the samurai. This death is doubly disturbing – partly because there is an implication that it is Kikuchiyo's fault for leaving his post and partly because the two are so closely connected in the film (is Yohei an alternative to Kanbei as a more realistic father figure for Kikuchiyo?).

Mosuke is the fourth villager in the group who travels to the town and a dissident voice amongst the farmers. He leads a revolt against Kanbei when he is ordered to abandon his house outside the village defences. But this challenge to collective responsibility is soon quashed. Gisaku is the old man who lives in the mill and provides the words of wisdom that drive the whole narrative. He has seen everything before and gets straight to the point of the farmers' problems: 'Hire hungry samurai.'

breechless beneath his armour

But if these are individuated characters, the villagers are generally represented as a 'mass'. Audie Bock (1978) argues that the moments of comedy and ridicule prevent the representation of the farmers 'from deteriorating into a Soviet-style people's film glorifying the peasantry'. This is presumably a reference to the so-called 'socialist realist' films of the 1930s when Stalin forced film makers into 'heroic' depictions of the masses. Kurosawa was much more likely to have been influenced by Eisenstein and Pudovkin's 1920s films with their array of striking faces to 'humanise' workers, soldiers and peasants in films like *Battleship Potemkin* (USSR 1925), *Mother* (USSR 1926) and *Storm over Asia* (USSR 1928).

As Bock suggests, the triumph of *Seven Samurai* is to present a narrative that is initiated by the community who emerge as the victors in a revolutionary move for Japanese cinema. The undoubted individual skills of the samurai are moulded into a collective weapon by the strategies deployed by Kanbei and are instrumental in the victory of the community. The theme of individual endeavour and collective good is a consistent aspect of Kurosawa's work.

THE BANDITS

A major difference between *Seven Samurai* and its American remake is in the depiction of the bandits. Where *The Magnificent Seven* offers a 'magnificent' villain in the form of Eli Wallach, Kurosawa's bandits are not individuated to any degree. We recognise a leader and we hear a few lines of dialogue that help to deliver plot information, but no names and little in the way of motivation.

A few of the bandits wear the elaborate armour which marks out a samurai general and others seem to bear some resemblance to the samurai defenders. One wears the long kimono of Kuzeo and another is breechless beneath his armour like Kikuchiyo. Does the bandit group include 'disgraced' or 'dishonoured' samurai, or have they, like the villagers, stolen the armour from dead samurai? Either way, there is certainly a suggestion that the faceless bandits are more disturbing in that they are almost like an evil mirror image of the defenders – a warning as to what the farmers and samurai might become without self-discipline and a collective ethos. They do act in a form of collective thuggery, but Kanbei's strategy is to pick them off in twos and threes, trapping them in the village and never confronting the forty en masse.

A NOTE ON TYPES

Typing is essential if there are many characters and little time to introduce them. Negative attitude towards types derives largely from the 'stereotype', a concept of a broadly drawn character representing an entire social group and used originally in social psychology. The repetition of some stereotypes across different media has been seen to foster prejudice against selected groups. But stereotypes need not be negative – it depends on the power relationships embedded in the stereotypical representation, i.e. if groups are stereotyped as criminal or victims by society as a whole.

Seven Samurai does not use stereotypes as such and it is clear that Kurosawa does not 'take sides'. The film exposes both the farmers and the samurai as guilty of reprehensible behaviour. But there are 'types' in the film. To a certain extent they are 'generic types' and thus possibly difficult for western audiences to read – i.e. the samurai are presented in opposition to the samurai type in traditional ***jidaigeki.*** But they are also 'archetypes' – characters constructed around universal values and recognisable across traditional forms of literature and theatre (literally the 'original model' of the character). Kanbei is an archetypal hero, Gisaku a wise man, Yohei a sad clown etc. Kurosawa's treatment of the script allows these archetypal figures to be presented with real human personalities.

narrative shape

Most film narratives can be defined as 'linear' or 'circular'. Action films tend towards linearity in that they are 'goal-orientated' with an identifiable 'quest' for a hero figure to achieve. Such narratives are about 'winning' – a philosophy easily recognisable in Hollywood films. Narratives that concern relationships in families or communities are better described as 'circular', since they are about building links between people and stressing the continuity of institutions, or at least their evolution. Education and re-education are more important in these narratives than winning a battle. Social comedies or melodramas might be good examples of such narratives, but it is worth noting that many traditional Hollywood genres like the Western exhibit a tension between the two types. Indeed a change of ending might shift the structure from one type to another. A stranger rides into town and defeats the bad guys who are terrorising the population. Does the film end with the stranger riding off into the sunset, goal achieved, or with the town getting on with normal life again and learning to be civilised?

Seven Samurai combines the two types. There is a clear goal to be achieved, but the resolution of the narrative suggests that it is perhaps more important to consider the re-education of Kikuchiyo and the return to the ritual of planting as the basis for civilised existence. This is emphasised in the reference to the seasons (the harvests and planting) and the cyclical nature of existence. This is not the American notion of 'progress' through achievement. The samurai have fought bravely, upholding their honour, but new bandits will return and the villagers will carry on planting and harvesting. It will be some time before the society begins to change. It is interesting to compare the cyclical nature of the story of *Seven Samurai* and that of *Ugetsu Monogatari*, Kenji Mizoguchi's film of 1953. This film is set in the same civil war period and tells the story of two peasant couples, potters rather than farmers. They have adventures but the film resembles a ghost story rather than an action film, and it starts and ends with the potter by his kiln. In Mizoguchi's case, however, the cyclical form is signified by a child and a grave in the final scene – a mother dies but a child grows up to take her place.

narrative time

Films are 'time-based' texts and they tell stories in 'cinematic space' as created through the application of visual and aural techniques. On a simple level, *Seven Samurai* organises narrative time according to the seasons. The opening sees the bandits deciding to wait until the barley harvest before attacking, having previously stolen the rice harvest. The barley is harvested, the bandits attack and are defeated and the film ends with the planting of the next rice crop.

The time scale is relatively short. We learn that the farmers have already been in the town for ten days before Kanbei appears and they worry that the barley near the town is nearly ready. Rikichi scolds them and points out that their own mountain barley will be later. When they return to the village there is time to prepare the defences and the battles that follow cover a few days. Kurosawa codes the passage of time with three different transitions. The conventional cut suggests simply a change of shot to another viewpoint in the same time period, whereas the slow fade to black and fade up to a new image suggests the passage of time, from several hours to several days. Somewhere between these two comes Kurosawa's trademark (in this period of film making), the swift horizontal **wipe** that is used on several occasions to jump forward a few minutes or perhaps an hour. This unique device allows Kurosawa to stress the urgency of the action, but to maintain a sense of narrative time passing.

One example of the use of the wipe comes at the end of the sequence when the farmers have almost given up hope of finding a samurai and they are brawling on the road. (This follows a fade signifying that this is the morning after their humiliation in the boarding house.) The speech by Rikichi discussed above then follows and the others agree to stay on. At this point the wipe is used, almost like a **jump cut** (see Style) to move the narrative forward to the same scene a little later when the farmers are washing their clothes, just as Kanbei appears at the head of a crowd of townspeople. The wipe suggests that having stayed on and committed themselves by spending time washing, their reward is to discover Kanbei.

On two other occasions, the wipe appears to be used for formal reasons, because it 'fits' the editing style. The first occasion is early in the film when the farmers have just arrived in the town and are observing the different samurai wandering through the streets. This is a brilliant sequence with fast cutting and use of a telephoto lens as the samurai stride across the screen one way in medium shot and the farmers look swiftly in the other direction. All the time, the townspeople are scurrying past in the foreground. With the blaring horns on the soundtrack, the pace of this sequence is exhilarating. Rikichi nods to suggest that they have seen a samurai to approach. But how can Kurosawa end the **montage** of swift cuts and show time passing? The wipe is inspired. It matches the cuts and as it moves across the screen it reveals a long shot of the crowd parting to allow a samurai to toss Rikichi aside and rebuke him for deigning to offer work.

The second such use of the wipe comes during the ride to the bandit's fort. This is a brilliant piece of editing, collapsing time and place into a seamless sequence. We are shown the four riders moving down into the valley in a long shot from the rear and then the wipe reveals them appearing by the waterfall. This is a sleight of hand, an effect only achievable through editing.

narrative space

Kurosawa constructed a village so that he could film as he wished. The village is located in a wooded valley in the mountains – an isolated community surrounded by trees and hills, almost mythical in its location. There are no casual passers-by coming through the village. There are four potential sites of action – the townscape, the village itself, the woods and the bandits' lair in the mountains in a rocky gorge. In themselves these are not unusual locations but they do offer the potential for different stories and they suggest different values.

The town, following some of the observations above, is a place of hustle and bustle, of meetings between different groups of people. We are shown characters striding purposefully in different directions. This is the 'modern' world and is distinguished from the quieter rural life of the village. The village and the bandit's lair are not totally dissimilar. Both are small communities built next to water, but the village is circled by fertile fields and woods, whereas the bandits are hemmed in by inhospitable rocks. There is something almost demonic about the bandits' lair (and the samurai appear to go down to find it). The woods are an ambiguous area between village and lair – they offer an area of beauty and recreation for the villagers, but also afford concealment to the marauding bandits. Katsushiro and Shino discover the three bandit scouts in the woods during their romantic tryst.

oppositions

structuring oppositions

Narratives are constructed around conflict – there is little interest in a story that doesn't involve struggle of some kind. The anthropologist Claude Lévi-Strauss studied myth-making in tribal cultures and suggested that the structuring principle in many tales could be studied through the concept of **'oppositions'** of ideas or values. This approach was first applied in film studies to Westerns (particularly those of John Ford). Here are some of the oppositions suggested for the Western by Jim Kitses:

Wilderness	Civilisation
the individual	the community
freedom	restriction
honour	institutions
self-knowledge	illusion
integrity	compromise
pragmatism	idealism
savagery	humanity
tradition	change
the past	the future

extracted from Kitses, 1969, p. 11

These oppositions refer to the themes of many Westerns and the depiction of conflicts between characters associated with the frontier/wilderness such as the Native Americans and the cowboy/trailhand or outlaw and those associated with the 'settlement' of the west. The oppositions immediately point to both the enormous range of potential stories and to the thematic richness and complexity of the Western, which is perhaps not surprising in a genre that deals directly with such a crucial period in American history. To take just one example, a Western narrative could be structured around the coming of the railroad which will make redundant the skills of the trailhand and restrict the freedom of men who will have to get jobs in town or work on a ranch.

Given Kurosawa's interest in American cinema and in the Western in

a landscape of mistrust, deceit, and pessimism

particular and also the status of the period film in Japanese culture, is this approach useful in exploring the themes of *Seven Samurai*? Certain oppositions in Kitses' list are still valid if we place the samurai on the left and the farmers on the right. Others don't work or are reversed. If nothing else, we've already questioned the simplified notion that the 'samurai picture' is just a Japanese version of the Western. The samurai are not interchangeable with the gunmen in Westerns (Kurosawa [1986] is quite dismissive of the Westerns made from his films: 'They are gangsters, not samurai!'). A complicating factor is Kurosawa's use of the bandits to represent a third group. How can the bandits be incorporated into a set of oppositions? Perhaps they should be treated as a faceless enemy, devoid of values and treated more like part of a malevolent environment? Or perhaps the samurai are the third force, coming between the farmers and the bandits (representing civilisation and the wilderness) and acting rather like the cavalry in Ford's Westerns?

The transposition from the Western to the *jidaigeki* – the period film – does not work partly because sixteenth-century Japan was not yet approaching industrialisation and therefore there is not the same theme of 'change' in the *jidaigeki*, even if it is being used to comment in some way on contemporary Japan (see Contexts). The samurai and the farmers are both part of a feudal system that will not change for some time to come. The oppositions therefore are more likely to come from the different ideas and values concerned with how to cope with the problems of the present. Robert Perry suggests that this is Kurosawa's most important theme:

> ...to know and to act are one and the same. From this the closest personae we can attribute to Kurosawa through his work is that of the samurai hero, often the ronin or masterless samurai; a man of action expelled from his previous vocation to walk a path of personal and spiritual enlightenment in a landscape of mistrust, deceit, and pessimism. This hero, often personified in the capable interpretations of actor Toshiro Mifune, then becomes Kurosawa's 'theme' with the reality of the environment counter-balancing his ethical code. Dualities of chaos/order, heroism/humanism, action/

oppositions

indifference, and most importantly, illusion/reality all come into play.

Perry, 1997, see bibliography websites

Perry suggests that the last of these four 'dualities' is the most important in *Seven Samurai*. Not only will the would-be samurai characters (Katsushiro and Kikuchiyo) learn 'to know and to act', but we too will go through a process of accepting an illusion and then becoming aware of reality. At the end of the film Kanbei's speech about the farmers being the real victors is evidence of his final wisdom – he accepts the outcome, knowing the danger of allowing the illusion (the unfulfilled wish 'to win') to supersede the reality (ungrateful peasants, dead comrades) (See Richie, 1996).

The film begins with chaos. The bandits, like a malevolent environmental force, throw the farmers into confusion – how will they avoid the next raid? Much of the film is taken up with the attempts by the samurai to instil 'order' into the behaviour of the villagers in defence of their homes and crops. Perry does not explain why he proposes action/indifference as a duality, but we can reasonably assume that he refers to both the selection of the samurai – those who are prepared to act rather than ignore the farmers – and to the farmers who must move towards 'action' if they are to save themselves. Then again, he may be referring to the 'push, pull' of Kurosawa's narrative with its periods of brisk action punctuated by periods of comedy and reflection. But underpinning both these structuring devices is the duality of illusion/reality.

At the beginning of the film, the audience accepts an illusion – there is a simple structure being set up of victims (farmers), villains (bandits) and heroes (samurai). This will persist until the discovery of the samurai armour and Kikuchiyo's speech. After this the audience is aware that both the farmers and the samurai can be deceitful. As the preparation for the bandits' attack gets underway, there is the development of another illusion – Kanbei has everything so well planned, nothing can go wrong, can it? The final battle reveals the horror of slaughter in the mud and the ending reveals the crucial illusion for the audience and the samurai – there is no victory, the farmers ignore them (and us).

oppositions narrative & form

the concept of the 'human nexus'

Perry also relates illusion/reality to the role of Kanbei, a truly Kurosawan 'hero'. The introduction of Kanbei is in itself a deception. He has his head shaved, signifying loss of status, a terrible act. Yet it is part of a deception to allow him to rescue a child – risking his life for no tangible reward. The expected hero of a traditional **chanbara** is revealed as something very different, the illusion of heroism is the reality of his humanism. Kurosawa said that he preferred his heroes to be modest men. Kikuchiyo, by contrast, is a braggart (but also capable of great humanity) and he must learn from Kanbei. Perry (1997) quotes sociologist Hajime Nakamura and the concept of the 'human nexus':

> The people to whom a human nexus is important place great moral emphasis upon complete and willing dedication of the self to others in a specific human collective. This attitude, though it may be a basic moral requirement in all peoples, occupies a dominant position in Japanese social life. Self-dedication to a specific human nexus has been one of the most powerful factors in Japanese history.
>
> *Hajime Nakamura, Ways of Thinking of Eastern Peoples,*
> *translated by Philip Weiner, Honolulu, East-West Center Press, 1964*

Perry goes on to relate this to 1950s' Japan by quoting Stephen Prince: '...breaking from these social groups [in this case the apathy of post-feudal Japan] to discover a regard for human dignity'. (Stephen Prince, *The Warrior's Camera: The Cinema of Akira Kurosawa*, New Jersey, Princeton University Press, 1991).

Kanbei, then, represents a humanist manifestation of the samurai warrior code. Through Kanbei's actions and their impact upon Kikuchiyo and Katsushiro, Kurosawa builds his narrative themes of individual/collective, heroism/humanism and illusion/reality.

style

Some films, action films especially, seem primarily concerned with narrative events, rather than the way in which they are presented. Other films emphasise presentation and visual or aural style at the expense of narrative development. It is immensely satisfying to find a film that is both exciting as a narrative and fascinating to watch. *Seven Samurai* is a film of renown within world cinema but it is also a Japanese film – a film from a country with a traditional aesthetic quite different from that in the west. This chapter begins with an attempt to 'place' Kurosawa in relation to Japanese culture.

japanese aesthetics & influences on cinema

A major issue in any discussion of Kurosawa's films – and of *Seven Samurai* in particular – is how to read them in terms of 'Japaneseness'. Alongside China and India, Japan offers a sustained history of aesthetic practice that to European sensibilities is clearly 'different'. Traditional Japanese art, music and theatre (i.e. pre-twentieth century) were not only 'about' different things, but they presented their worlds in different ways. Cinema, as the art form of the twentieth century and the 'industrial age', offers the possibility of creating a universal language of sounds and images, but the extent to which national cinemas are differentiated by the traditional arts on which they draw for inspiration remains an issue. Kurosawa was criticised for being in some way too American or too 'western' by commentators in Japan, but in the west his films were clearly seen as Japanese. What does it mean to be 'Japanese' in this sense and how does it help our understanding of *Seven Samurai*?

The history of Japanese painting is an obvious reference point. Sato Tadao

cherry blossom, the crane and the pine tree

(1994) makes a useful distinction between different types of painting and points to ways in which a particular subject matter may create different meanings in Japanese and western art. For instance, a landscape in European painting may be 'romantic' in representing the beauty of the natural world or it may signify the wealth of the artist's patron or simply represent a familiar location. In Japanese art, images of mountains and especially running water are more likely to be signifiers of spiritual values – the mountains invoke Taoist ideas about the places where immortals dwell and rivers and lakes refer to Buddhist principles of flux and impermanence. Images of Mount Fuji, snow to evoke purity and other natural symbols such as the sun and moon occur frequently in traditional painting and also in the compositions of the older generation of directors such as Ozu and Mizoguchi. They are not so prevalent in Kurosawa's work, which Tadao suggests is because he belongs to a younger generation.

'Bird and flower' paintings were commissioned by rich lords from the six- teenth to the eighteenth centuries. They drew on even older traditions of using landscapes and images from the natural world to produce decorative art for wealthy residences (rather than the 'ancestor portraiture' of wealthy Europeans). Such paintings incorporated images of the seasons, including cherry blossom, the crane and the pine tree, representing in turn 'transience and evanescence', longevity and good fortune. Kurosawa does occasionally use these symbols in composition and Tadao points out that in a composition from *Rashomon* he was the first Japanese director to shoot the sun, filtering it through leaves. In *Seven Samurai* the carpet of flowers found by the young lovers has a deep resonance for a Japanese audience.

Specific styles of Japanese painting have had an influence on cinema. ***Emaki*** were long scroll paintings 'read' from right to left (as Japanese script is read) as the scroll was unfurled. The same figures and locations re- occur in the scroll, at a uniform size and seen slightly from above, enabling a narrative to be constructed. Kenji Mizoguchi developed a cinema style involving a tracking camera that produced continuous long shots from a slightly high angle. This style, evident particularly in *Ugetsu Monogatari* (1953), helped Mizoguchi to earn the title of 'painterly'. There are moments when Kurosawa adopts slightly high angles, but often he favours cutting rather than long takes.

disparity between standing and sitting positions

There is one aspect of Kurosawa's style that could be related to traditional Japanese architecture – his swift horizontal wipe matches the sliding doors of Japanese houses. The Japanese custom of sleeping and sitting on futons and tatami mats rather than on beds and furniture means that characters in domestic scenes are much lower in the **frame** and that there is more disparity between standing and sitting positions. The result is that compared to conventional Hollywood studio practice of maintaining a mid shot throughout an indoor scene, Japanese directors have had to re-think camera angles and compositions. Tadao comments on the prevalence of low-angle shots in Yasujiro Ozu's films. He relates them to one of the relatively few schools of Japanese portraiture in which subjects would often be viewed from a low angle 'conveying a sense of grandeur'. Again, Ozu's very static style seems very different from Kurosawa's, but such shots are not unknown in the indoor scenes in *Seven Samurai*, and *Kagemusha* (1980) begins with a very long static shot recalling such paintings with their geometrical composition.

During the **Edo era** a technological innovation – the mass production of prints using wood blocks – had a profound effect on Japanese visual culture. These prints (*ukiyo-e*) were designed for a 'middle market' of merchants and samurai rather than the aristocracy – a modern mass market, comparable to the 'postcard' culture in Europe after the invention of photography. *Ukiyo-e* covered a wide range of subjects. Popular prints featured entertainers and courtesans, sumo matches, temples and other places of interest. Some prints were openly erotic in appeal. These images made use of the idea of perspective, brought in from the west and for the first time Japanese images conveyed a sense of depth. Compositions in depth became a feature carried over into cinema, often emphasised by objects in the foreground, requiring **deep focus** photography (see below).

Two very famous Japanese artists emerged at the start of the nineteenth century. Katsushika Hokusai produced images of Mount Fuji and the now famous image of a tidal wave, and Utagawa Hiroshige produced narrative series such as the story of the traditional journey from Kyoto to Edo. According to the website of The Virtual Museum of Traditional Japanese Art: 'The emotive tenor of works by these two artists has resonated deeply with

use of perspective

東海道
五拾三次
之内
御油
旅人留女

This woodblock print by Hiroshige
shows the use of perspective and
'deep' composition as taken up by
Kurosawa. The image depicts the
inns at Goyu, one of the '53 Stages
of the Tokaido' (the road from
Kyoto to Edo).

the Japanese sensitivity and their works are still widely loved and appreciated' (http://jin.jcic.or.jp/museum/).

Mizoguchi made at least one film about such artists (*Utamaro and his Five Women*, 1947) and it is clear that all Japanese film directors must have been influenced in some way by *ukiyo-e*. Tadao points out that the prints were important in representing the two extremes of Japanese masculinity. Samurai were not supposed to be 'weakened' by ideas of romance and were to be represented as strong and heroic. But the market wanted romance and eroticism, so new images appeared of men who were beautiful, but also effeminate and emotionally and physically weak. Tadao suggests that Mizoguchi selected heroes like Utamaro who were 'weak' and Kurosawa tended towards the 'strong'. In *Seven Samurai* this distinction is used to reinforce the sense of master/pupil between Kanbei and Katsushiro and also between Kikuchiyo, Kanbei and Katsushiro. Katsushiro is young, beautiful and compared to the others emotionally and physically weak (until his first 'kill'). Kikuchiyo is physically strong, but shows his emotional weakness with the children.

Richie (1994), writing for the same collection as Tadao, takes a slightly different tack. He points out that whereas in the west, cinema drew directly from photography and the 'realism' of nineteenth-century painting, in Japan early cinema was more dependent on the 'look' of traditional theatre in which realism was less important. Painting was an influence in Japan but in a different way. Two key aspects of the influence of European painting styles on western cinema are 'lighting' and treatment of space to connote 'psychological movement'. Western film makers often refer to the concept of painting or moulding scenes with light, so lighting conventions became an integral part of staging scenes and composing images. Richie suggests that the **Kabuki theatre** was uninterested in light and shadow and quickly adopted electric lamps as a means of banishing shadows – thus a tendency for Japanese cinema to opt for 'high key' lighting, evenly balanced to present a 'flat', brightly-lit image.

Space itself was treated differently in Japan where the idea of 'empty' space has to be constructed through artistic expression. Richie suggests that a blank sheet of paper does not suggest emptiness until a mark is made on it – emptiness has to be defined. Japanese compositions may then balance the empty and the 'filled' parts of the image. In the west, 'empty' might connote 'absent', but this is not the same meaning as 'empty' for Japanese. Richie points to other subtle differences in compositions, such as the effect of reading right to left in Japan. A diagonal composition running bottom left to top right suggests climbing, striving in the west, but descending in Japan.

Several of Richie's points are underpinned by a distinction he uses, drawn from a seventeenth-century Japanese treatise on aesthetics. This suggests that a painting that is good because it is 'lifelike' draws on the 'laws of life', whereas a painting that is good because it is not lifelike is drawing on the 'rules of art'. He refers to this distinction in a discussion of framing, suggesting that in the west, film makers consider that a dramatic scene is usually 'filled' and that the frame helps to 'cut out' certain aspects of the action, focusing attention. Certain Japanese film makers (and here he includes Kurosawa alongside Ozu and Mizoguchi) consider that there is no scene until a frame has been created – then it is a question of placing action in the frame, creating a reality which is 'closed and composed'. Here is cinema following the 'laws of art'. Richie goes on to link this to a general sense of film making that is 'anthropomorphic' – that takes art to be something created by the human mind and not by natural forces. He refers to a culture where the notion of beauty in a Japanese garden is bound up with the human intervention in moving a stone or a plant.

These discussions about Japanese painting are also applicable to other aspects of Japanese aesthetics, including the theatre (see Context) and music and poetry. Music is explored later in this section. The best known form of Japanese poetry in the west is the **_haiku_**, an epigrammatic seven-teen-syllable poem summing up a single idea. Alongside other traditional aesthetic modes of expression such as **_ikebana_** (flower arranging) and landscape gardening, Japanese poetry points to an aesthetic less concerned with the 'representational' or with the 'realism' of western art.

kurosawa & japanese aesthetics

In the discussion above, Kurosawa emerges with a practice both related to traditional aesthetics and sometimes consciously opposed to them. For many critics he comes out as significantly less 'painterly' and 'Japanese' than Kenji Mizoguchi and is valued less for this reason. Is this view reasonable or even sensible?

Kurosawa was indeed trained in 'western painting techniques' and his images are composed in depth with highly developed use of lighting and an obvious relationship to the realism of both painting and photography. This perfectly complements his selection of narrative structures, reproducing the effects of the American Westerns that he loved, and makes his films more easily understood in the west. But this doesn't immediately make him less 'Japanese' (and certainly not less 'painterly' – indeed, it could be argued that Kurosawa is one of the most painterly film makers of the twentieth century, maintaining his keen eye for composition developed in his youth as a putative artist.)

The confusion over Kurosawa's work is related to the history of Japanese cultural and educational practice in the **Meiji** and **Taisho eras**. As Sato (1994) points out, Japanese governments began to bring western ideas about art, music and drama into the education system during the Meiji era towards the end of the nineteenth century. They believed that Japan could only compete against the western powers if it embraced their ideas and jettisoned traditional Japanese ideas. In Context there is a brief discussion of the early history of the Japanese cinema and the way in which western and traditional Japanese forms were brought together. American and European films were widely seen in Japan and influenced the development of Japanese genres, as the early cinema based on traditional theatrical forms came to be modified. In his mix of the Western and traditional Japanese culture, Kurosawa was profoundly 'Japanese' – but his keen eye created something more distinctive from the mix, a style more aware of the power of western aesthetics.

---

revolutionary

Far from moving away from Japanese traditions, Kurosawa was one of the main innovators, bringing a sense of 'real' history to the popular *jidaigeki* or 'costume' pictures. Kurosawa undertook extensive research into costume and social behaviour in sixteenth-century Japan and far from Americanising a traditional Japanese story, in *Seven Samurai* he presented a more 'authentic' view of Japanese history. Elsewhere in his work, Kurosawa made use of traditional forms where they served his narrative purposes. In his adaptation of *Macbeth* (*Throne of Blood*, 1957) he encouraged his 'Lady Macbeth' to adopt the acting style of traditional **Noh theatre.** Later he adapted Shakespeare's *King Lear* for *Ran* (1985) and also drew on Russian literature, including both Gorky (*The Lower Depths*) and Dostoyevsky (*The Idiot*). All these adaptations were thoroughly Japanese in their settings and Kurosawa was determined to explore Japanese stories, even when he borrowed narrative structures. His two ventures abroad for the abortive *Tora! Tora!* (1969) and the more successful *Dersu Uzala* (1975) were forced on him by lack of finance at home. Significantly, Kurosawa's example has convinced the leading Chinese director of the 1990s, Zhang Yimou, to 'stay and make my films in China'. In any view of Kurosawa's cinema, either its thematic content or its style , it would be wrong to suggest that it is not 'Japanese'.

seven samurai & style

Seven Samurai is a film of its period but also a film that is revolutionary in its visual style, sound and editing. This can make it a confusing film for modern audiences trying to identify its stylistic features. To make an obvious point, here is an 'epic' film that deserves consideration alongside the best action adventure films of the late twentieth century, but one that uses few of the technologies available to modern cinema. In particular it is photographed in black and white, in **Academy ratio** (i.e. before the introduction of modern 'widescreen') and carries a mono soundtrack. Yet it creates as much narrative excitement as any widescreen Technicolor epic in Dolby Stereo. Such is Kurosawa's skill, not only in editing, which he supervised himself, but also in encouraging and working closely with his team, including cinematographer Asakazu Nakai and composer Fumio Hayasake.

The continuing popularity of *Seven Samurai* depends as much on Kurosawa's skill in utilising a wide range of cinematic techniques as it does on his undoubted ability to tell a story. As many critics have noted, *Seven Samurai* is above all an entertaining film that never flags over its long running time. Interest is maintained because Kurosawa knows how to energise each frame through movement, even if sometimes it is only a quivering lip or nostril in a close-up (Richie, 1996). The pent-up energy in the frame begs to be released and adds to the intensity of the action sequences.

Kurosawa was an innovator and a perfectionist. He understood and was able to employ all the techniques that the relatively impoverished Japanese studios of the early 1950s could offer. Some basic discussion of filming techniques is necessary in order to demonstrate how Kurosawa maximised their effect

visual style

SCREEN RATIOS

The standard screen ratio of 1.33:1 was established around 1930 when films began to carry an optical soundtrack, losing a small amount of the available print area on 35mm filmstock previously available for 'silent films'. The new standard became known as 'Academy'.

'Widescreen' formats, using either a 'squeezed' wide image on a standard gauge of film or a bigger film gauge, had been invented in the late 1920s, but their full introduction was delayed, mainly because of the extra costs facing cinemas in a time of economic recession. The first 'universal' widescreen process, CinemaScope, was introduced in the US and Europe by Twentieth Century Fox in 1953. The new format had an original screen ratio of 2.55:1, later reduced to 2.35:1, and introduced a wholly new look to cinema, utilised first for epic and spectacular pictures. The new technology did not become available to Japanese film makers straight away and Kurosawa did not use widescreen until the late 1950s.

The new screen shape allowed those directors, who could adapt, to compose shots differently. It offered a wider screen image, but one that was sometimes not so high (partly because of difficulties of fitting the new

visual style style

screens into cinemas). Nevertheless, there was generally more space available in the frame and the extra width allowed new compositions such as two characters together in the frame with space between, or two or three separate sites of action within the same frame. Overall, it meant a 'panoramic' view of cinema, emphasising width more than height in the image. By the 1960s and the introduction of variable Panavision lenses, the Academy ratio had disappeared and all films had 'widened' to a minimum in Hollywood of 1.85:1 ('modern widescreen') with occasional forays, mostly for 'blockbusters', into ratios of 2.35:1. The Academy ratio is roughly equivalent to the standard television screen, so films shot on Academy can be shown 'full screen' without any loss of the picture area on video. All modern films must be either **'panned** and scanned', showing only part of the widescreen image at any one time, or 'letterboxed', showing something like the correct shape, but with blank video above and below the image.

This explanation of changing screen ratios is necessary in order to understand two points. The first is the confusion of audiences for the video and DVD versions of *Seven Samurai,* some of whom have complained that the print is 'panned and scanned' and how disgraceful it is that we can't see the full screen image. There is a general assumption that *Seven Samurai* must be a widescreen epic – but it isn't. The second point that follows on from this is that Kurosawa must have found a way to compensate for the lack of width by use of other cinematic techniques.

Since cinema is (most of the time) a two-dimensional medium representing a three-dimensional world, one obvious answer is to use the 'other' dimension of height and Kurosawa's use of the relatively 'tall' Academy frame is discussed below. But although cinema is only two dimensional, it does offer the illusion of a third dimension in 'depth of field', the depth of the 'plane of action' and Kurosawa exploited this to the full, effectively extending the standard plane (i.e. action takes place in the 'middle ground') to include characters moving to and from the background and also across the foreground. In this way, Kurosawa was able to increase the amount of action within the Academy frame and allied to his editing skill and shooting techniques this provided the means to revolutionise action cinema.

BLACK & WHITE CINEMATOGRAPHY

As with widescreen, Japanese directors were unable to use colour processes such as Technicolor (or the homegrown Fujicolor) on a regular basis until the mid 1950s (modern colour cinematography was introduced on selected films in the late 1930s in Hollywood). Kurosawa did not make a colour film until *Dodeska'den* in 1970. Again the black and white work of the 1940s and 1950s presents a problem for modern audiences, for whom it is equated with what is seen as the 'arty' use of black and white in advertisements and attempts to invoke the 'glamour' of traditional **film noir.** Black and white is now an expensive option for film-makers, but in the 1950s it was the norm.

Two points are worth considering. First, modern video copies of 1950s' films rarely do justice to the luminous quality of the black and white cinema prints that appeared on first release. (It is well worth going to cinema screenings of new prints of black and white films – but they must be new prints, remastered from original negatives, not simple copies of existing prints). Black and white photography is able to achieve much better definition than most colour film (and this was certainly true in the 1950s) and through careful use of lighting can produce incredibly beautiful and detailed images, benefiting from increased contrast with velvety black shadows and glowing whites. Black and white in the hands of a skilled cinematographer can be 'richer' in tone than colour.

Partly because of this quality of the image, audiences in the 1950s were more inclined to accept black and white films as 'realist' (compared to what were often garishly coloured musicals and costume epics). The reverse is now true, but *Seven Samurai* was seen as a 'realist' film and the images of the town and village are certainly similar to those achieved in the **neo-realist** work of Satyajit Ray in 1955 with the first of his 'Apu' films based on the life of a Bengal village boy. Neo-realism refers to the practices adopted by some Italian film makers from the early 1940s and can be traced further back to the work of Jean Renoir in the late 1930s in France. The main visual requirement of neo-realism was location shooting and *Seven Samurai* qualifies on this basis – Kurosawa was again an innovator in making this kind of film on location in the mountains rather than on a

simple images carrying profound meaning

Kyoto studio lot. Neo-realism was the dominant visual style of most of what was considered 'art cinema' in Europe in the 1950s, and this is another reason why *Seven Samurai* was so accessible to European audiences.

Neo-realism is a philosophy focusing on representing the world as it is (using non-actors and scripts based on everyday events – criteria that disqualify *Seven Samurai*). But it still allows for some expressive moments and there are shots in *Seven Samurai* that seem at first sight to be redundant in terms of advancing the narrative. Some of these may derive from particular Japanese aesthetics (see the first part of this chapter). The sequences showing the flowers in the forest may fit into this category, although it is possible to explain these in terms of the growing relationship between the young lovers and on another occasion the serenity of the swordsman, Kuzeo, who lies amongst the flowers, seemingly at peace. More enigmatic is the shot in the early part of the film, immediately after Rikichi has been humiliated by the samurai whom he has approached to help. The new sequence starts with the rain and a static shot in which an object hangs in a porch in the foreground in sharp focus, while in the background, slightly blurred, two peasants walk down the road in long shot. What is the object – a scabbard for a short sword, a pair of rope sandals? It is hard to distinguish. It is not uncommon in Japanese imagery to be presented with relatively simple images carrying profound meaning, but such shots are relatively rare in Kurosawa's work. This composition, inexplicable in terms of content, is however recognisable as a conventional shot in terms of composition.

FRAMING AND COMPOSITION

Whatever appears on screen will usually (but not always) have been scripted and to this extent is a 'given' – it needs to be shown. But there are a myriad of ways in which any person or object can be visualised. **Framing** refers to the 'size' and the general position of the subject in the frame. The world looks very different through the viewfinder of the camera and the director's task is to decide on a strategy for framing that fits the material. In studio production, some of these decisions can become highly conventional with directors told to shoot the same scene with different framings (to 'cover' the shots and give a choice to the editor). Working in a way to challenge studio conventions, Kurosawa was able to develop his own particular style of framing.

Composition refers more to the 'shape' of objects in the frame and to the proportions of the different parts of the image. Ideas about composition do refer back to more traditional ideas about composition in fine art, i.e. notions of beauty in the west are often associated with the 'rule of thirds' – the division of an image into notional thirds which 'balance' each other. Kurosawa had a possible advantage in composition because of his training in western art as well as his experience of traditional Japanese imagery.

Framing and composition in *Seven Samurai* are carefully developed in a coherent overall aesthetic. Since one of the major themes of the film is the relationship between individual and collective action, it is not surprising that the 'economy' of shots in the film is dependent to a large extent on long shots and close-ups.

Shot sizes are usually defined in terms of the presentation of the human body with the long shot showing the whole body, the medium or mid shot 'cutting off' the body at the waist and the close-up offering just the head and neck. Other shots are variations on these three. Sometimes the long shot is used to isolate an individual against a landscape for a particular reason, but at other times it will be used functionally, simply to be able to frame a 'crowd shot' – many people in a shot together. *Seven Samurai* must be partly shot in this way in order to present the villagers as a 'mass'.

Kurosawa's interest in the work of John Ford and the way it merges with traditional Japanese aesthetics is evident in compositions utilising dramatic skies. 'Large' skies with boiling, rolling clouds are evident in Kurosawa's first film *Sanshiro sugata* and they recur in *Seven Samurai*. Kurosawa's skies are often full of wind and rain while Ford's are more likely to be clear. The other noticeable difference is in the composition, with Ford arranging the skyline two thirds of the way down the frame for Western vistas. The opening of *Seven Samurai* moves from this Fordian image to show the skyline two thirds up the frame, as the bandits make their appearance. The skyline is often high in *Seven Samurai*, since the defenders of the village are constantly looking up to the mountains from where the attacks will come.

visual style

The skyline is high

The bandits appear on the skyline at
the start of the first battle. The
skyline is high as Kikuchiyo is
looking up. 'Reading' from right to
left, as a Japanese spectator might,
continues the move 'up'.

visual style

SHOOTING IN DEPTH

The use of objects in the foreground and a sense of depth in an image were relatively late features of Japanese painting (see reference to **ukiyo-e** in the first part of the chapter). Similar compositions in photography required the development of lenses and fast filmstock so that a tiny aperture could produce a 'deep' field of focus – objects in the foreground, middle ground and background all in sharp focus. Such compositions became possible in Hollywood in the late 1930s, not least in the films of John Ford (e.g. *Stagecoach* in 1939), and in the 1940s they became associated with a new approach to realism in the work of Orson Welles and William Wyler. André Bazin suggested that by allowing action in different parts of the 'stage' – i.e. the depth of the image – and shooting in long takes, film makers could allow the audience to decide which action to follow and how to link the action together, just as they would do in 'real' observation. Conventional editing 'chops up' the space and underlines the relationship between characters in a scene through the juxtaposition of shots.

In *Seven Samurai*, Kurosawa uses both the 'compositions in depth' associated with Welles and Wyler and the **montage** techniques of Eisenstein. This is noticeable in the scenes staged in the relatively confined spaces of the huts in the town and in the village. The scenes in the town use depth to great advantage. The crucial scene in which Kanbei accepts the job of defending the village starts with a long shot into the boarding house. In the foreground are the labourers who are still taunting the farmers. In the middle ground are the four farmers and standing behind them, Kanbei and Katsushiro. Behind them, clearly visible and in focus, we can see the life of the town going on as people pass in the street. Katsushiro reacts to the taunting and picks up his sword. Most of the sequence is covered in long shot, panning swiftly as Katsushiro chases the labourers and Kanbei tries to stop him. But dramatic close-ups of Katsushiro, his sword, and Kanbei are cut into the action as the labourers run round the room. Then one of the labourers hands a bowl of rice to Kanbei, pointing out that the farmers are eating millet in order to save the rice for the samurai. As Kanbei accepts the bowl and says to the farmers that he will accept their sacrifice, the bowl of rice is large in the foreground whilst the farmers cower against the far wall in the background. The whole scene makes perfect

visual style

the connection to the cowering villagers

Kanbei: 'I accept your sacrifice'. The
deep focus allows Kurosawa to place
the bowl in the foreground and make
the connection to the cowering
villagers more explicit. The town can
be seen going about its business
through the gaps in the wall of the hut.

narrative sense through composition, framing, camera movement, editing and the positioning of the actors. This short scene is perfect cinema – and it is only one of many such throughout the film.

The use of depth in the image compensates for the lack of width and Kurosawa uses the extra space to emphasise the differences between groups of characters by placing them at different distances from the camera. This is evident in the early scenes in which the villagers come across Kanbei in the town helping to rescue a baby from a bandit. The townspeople and the villagers watch in a group, standing in a **tableau** (again as in Ford) long shot, but sometimes shown in close mid shot. Peering over them is the young Katsushiro and in front, on his own, is Kikuchiyo. All are in focus, but in different 'planes' of the image. When Kanbei goes to the house, Kikuchiyo again runs to the front and grabs a bucket to sit on – he is now in the foreground as we watch Kanbei at work in the background. In the final part of the sequence, the villagers follow Kanbei on the road out of town and we watch from behind the villagers as Kikuchiyo runs through the depth of the image, past the villagers and up to Kanbei. Earlier, Kurosawa has emphasised the connections by giving us close-ups of Kikuchiyo watching Kanbei and a reverse close-up showing Kanbei looking at Kikuchiyo.

Shooting in depth is less common in contemporary cinema where a shallow depth of a field is often used to emphasise an object in the frame (i.e. it is in focus and everything else is blurred). Dramatic moments may see the focus shift from foreground to middle ground in the same shot.

VERTICAL FRAMINGS

The other way to compensate for the lack of widescreen is to make full use of the height of the Academy frame. A good example of this comes with the final acceptance of Kikuchiyo into the group. He travels with the six and while they watch from a cliff above a waterfall, he catches a fish with his bare hands below. Then, as they march along a wooded path and turn to face the camera, they wonder where he has got to. The composition here is vertical with the straight limbs of the trees leading the eye upwards. Kikuchiyo suddenly emerges behind the group, in the top of the frame, shouting and brandishing his sword. Similar scenes are common in

visual style

he suddenly appears

On their way to the village the six
samurai think that Kikuchiyo has
given up his attempt to join them, but
he suddenly appears ahead of them on
the path. With the samurai walking
into the background, 'up' the frame,
this is a good example of how
Kurosawa uses the height of the frame.

visual style

the village location, using the natural slopes. In one scene during a battle, action across the bottom of the screen runs left to right and at the top of the screen, another combat is pursued right to left. It is also noticeable that the village cemetery is a large mound with the samurai graves at the top and the path below. When Kikuchiyo sits by Gorobei's grave, perhaps believing that he is responsible for the death, he is in the top of the frame, but the main group is in the bottom of the frame – the vertical composition using the cemetery appears several times, not least at the end of the film.

ANGLES & DIAGONALS

Both high and low angles are found in traditional Japanese painting (see above) and they are deployed in traditional ways by Kurosawa in *Seven Samurai*. As Katsushiro walks with Kanbei after the formation of the group, the camera tracks them at a low angle, emphasising the power assigned to Kanbei. But when Kikuchiyo arrives to ask to join, the camera moves to a high angle seemingly supporting the aggressive and stronger man. With Kanbei's refusal of his offer, the angle drops again emphasising Kanbei's control. In the other scenes dealing only with the villagers, the camera is usually at eye level, unless it needs to move for dramatic emphasis. Diagonal lines in a composition are often said to signify 'disturbance' or conflict. This is true at a formal level and a 'calm' landscape is easily disturbed (and made more interesting) by the branch of a tree cutting across the straight line of the horizon. A striking feature of the village preparations for battle is the use of long bamboo spears by the farmers. Once they are armed in this way, every crowd shot produces a bristling of diagonals that intensify the sense of anticipation of the battle.

WILD WEATHER

Can there be another film maker who has used the elements as effectively and consistently in creating a sense of mood and location? Andrei Tarkovsky with his use of rain might be one contender, but for Kurosawa wind and rain are like another character in the narrative – he was so fond of the wind machine that his crew gave him the nickname 'wind man'. The masterstroke was to film the final battle in torrential rain. Along with the shooting and editing style, this is the reason the battle is so celebrated.

visual style

brilliant choreography of action

The first battle provides evidence of Kurosawa's
brilliant choreography of action and use of
composition and framing. The diagonals in this
image emphasise the conflict. The villagers are
pursuing one bandit, left to right in the bottom half
of the frame when suddenly another bandit gallops
across the top half of the frame, right to left.

visual style

The rain has varied effects – it helps to point to the realism of the combat, it intensifies the visual sense of mayhem and it encourages the motion in the image with sliding and splashing in the mud and pools. It also allows greater distinction to be made between the battle and its aftermath.

MAPS & SCOREBOARD

Film narratives are constructed in time and space. Often it is difficult to work out the 'geography' of the action. Kurosawa makes it very easy by presenting a map of the village, drawn up by Kanbei to enable the planning of the defence. This is presented as a close up following a high-angle shot looking down on Kanbei and his lieutenants as he inspects the village. Added to the map is a primitive 'scoreboard' on which Kanbei records the deaths of each bandit, enabling him to plan precisely how many to expect in each raiding party and whom to deploy against them. This is a much more effective way of presenting important plot information than using dialogue alone. It also allows Kurosawa to emphasise Kanbei's professionalism and military experience.

MIFUNE'S ACTING

Toshiro Mifune's introduction to acting is described in Background. Mifune's acting style is 'large' and in *Seven Samurai* includes a wide range of leaps, gestures, cries, laughs etc. Next to the still Kuzeo, the nervous young Katsushiro, the calm and authoritative Kanbei, Mifune's Kikuchiyo is almost like a cartoon figure, bouncing around the frame, playing for laughs but always the focus for attention. Mifune's performance becomes an element of the visual design – a focus for composition.

LIGHTING

There is relatively little to say about the lighting in the film except that as far as possible the lighting effect is 'natural'. It is enhanced for dramatic effect and modelled to serve the compositions, but generally interiors are dark, the sun filters through the trees and the village square is filled with dusty sunshine or pounding rain. In short, the lighting conforms to the **neo-realist** aesthetic of the period in international cinema.

three cameras shooting simultaneously

MULTI-CAMERA SHOOTING

Although most of *Seven Samurai* was shot conventionally with a single camera, the use of three cameras shooting simultaneously during the final battle was an important innovation. Later in the 1950s a new generation of Hollywood directors with experience of television (where studio drama production was invariably 'multi-camera') would use this practice consistently. In 1954 it was relatively new. Kurosawa's decision was largely pragmatic. If he had shot the battle with a single camera, it would have been very difficult to shoot the same sequence from different angles (i.e. moving the camera and re-staging the action). The likelihood was that when a sequence was repeated, the action (a horse galloping, swordfights in the background etc.) would be slightly different, making cutting between different shots difficult. Three cameras in different locations around the battle shooting simultaneously solved this problem by enabling cutting between angles. This shooting style also created a sense of spontaneity about the camerawork.

Shooting with three cameras is not straightforward to organise and Kurosawa worked with a limited number of cinematographers and camera operators who, he knew, could cope. 'The three camera positions are completely different for the beginning and end of each shot, and they go through several transformations in between. As a general system, I put the A camera in the most orthodox positions, use the B camera for quick, decisive shots and the C camera as a kind of guerilla unit' (Kurosawa, 1983)

TELEPHOTO

A **telephoto** ('long') lens allows distant images to be brought close to the viewer. Compared to a standard lens it 'distorts' by squashing the dead ground between the camera and the subject. (A wide-angle lens does the opposite, pushing the subject away from the camera and showing a wider spread of action.) Contemporary television uses telephoto lenses in news and sports coverage and such compositions have now become 'normal', but although long lenses had been introduced in the cinema in the early twentieth century, they were not often used in Hollywood until the 1960s. Partly this was because with studio shooting, directors were able to use dollies and cranes to move the camera close to the action. Kurosawa was once again an innovator in using a telephoto lens during the battle scenes in order to put the spectator into the battle.

The 'length' of the lens has implications for depth of field and light requirements. It is more likely to deliver a relatively shallow depth of field and this may be how Kurosawa achieves one of the striking sequences in the film. When the samurai first arrive in the village and Kikuchiyo sets off the alarm, each of the other samurai is shown running, left to right centre frame. They are shot centre frame in medium long shot held by a panning camera, but only the samurai figure is in focus. Each samurai is shown for only a few frames, each in the same position, almost as if they were a single figure. This brilliant sequence serves a dual purpose, to signify speed and motion (i.e. to emphasise action) and also to suggest that the six samurai are a collective force.

Elsewhere in the film, the compositions emphasise the pressure on the villagers and the samurai with 'tight' framings, often in depth. It is not always possible to tell which lens has been used since similar effects can be achieved with different combinations of lens, aperture and lighting, but the 'claustrophobia' sometimes associated with telephoto work is apparent and there is little of the distortion that would come from wide-angle lenses (as used in the **deep focus** work of Welles, for instance).

SLOW MOTION

Seven Samurai is famous for the slow motion shot in the sequence in which Kanbei rescues the child in the town. He enters the shed and a few moments later the thief stumbles out and then pitches towards his death in a slow fall. There is time for Kanbei to emerge and throw down the bloody sword, before the thief finally crumples into the dust which gently rises around him. There are various readings of this pivotal scene, avidly watched by the farmers and Katsushiro and Kikuchiyo. The slow motion freezes and emphasises the moment of death. It is both a measure of Kanbei's calm and methodical approach, his startling skill and professionalism and also a stark demonstration of the reality of death – a life literally stilled.

Various commentators have also noted slow motion shots during the climactic battle sequence. Weddle (1996) claims that Sam Peckinpah's

claustrophobic tension and momentary triumph

interest in using slow motion derives from seeing the battle scenes in *Seven Samurai* and refers specifically to the falling samurai. It may be that Peckinpah's practised eye could discern a change in film speed better than most, or it may be that such shots have been excised from current prints, but it is difficult to see what he meant. Certainly the deaths of Kyuzo and Kikuchiyo are drawn out, but they don't compare to the earlier use of slow motion. Now we have the advantage of replaying scenes on video, the whole battle scene is revealed to have a number of 'mistakes' in the editing. There are various **jump cuts** – unconventional cuts on the same action or cuts between different, but similarly sized shots of the same subject – and Kuzeo begins his fall before the shot actually rings out. But these don't matter in the mêlée and don't in any way detract from the brilliance of the sequence.

The crucial factor in shooting the battle scene is the use of more than one camera and when Peckinpah did attempt to go 'one better' he 'over-cranked' some of the six cameras he used on *The Wild Bunch*. Slow motion is achieved by running the film at 36 or 48 or more frames per second (fps) and then projecting at 24 fps, allowing the same action to take longer on screen. Kurosawa's innovation opened up a whole new range of possibilities for action.

TRANSITIONS

A distinctive transition device in the film is the rapid horizontal **wipe** (see Narrative & Form). Along with the careful staging in depth, tracking camera and **montage** of close-ups and tight shots mixed with long shots, the wipe motion keeps up the intensity of the narrative drive while still signifying time passing. Longer time elapses are signified by fades to black.

SUMMARY

Only a book-length shot analysis could do full justice to the richness of Kurosawa's style. From the brief comments above it should be possible to get an overall sense of action and anticipation, of claustrophobic tension and momentary triumph, all expressed through cinematography. The undoubted power of the images comes through some relatively simple devices. For instance, the close-ups of characters' faces have great impact, partly because they are so tightly framed with the top of the head close to the top of the frame, and the face shown from high or low angle. Secondly Kurosawa fills the frame with close-ups, often cramming two or more conventional close-ups or medium close-ups into the same composition, making full use of depth of field and the height of the frame. This effect is most pronounced with the groups of farmers, especially in the town in the 'searching sequence' when two farmers' heads turn to follow samurai marching past in the opposite direction. Each of these close-up or medium close-up pairs has a sweep of townsfolk passing in front of the camera.

If framing and composition in depth are the keys to interiors, the use of telephoto, slow motion, multiple camera and rapid panning typifies some of the outdoor action scenes.

music & sound

The use of music in Kurosawa's films deserves more attention than it generally receives. Two points can be made immediately. Western music is a generic feature of Japanese films, but scores in Kurosawa films use an effective mix of orchestral western music and traditional Japanese instrumentation. The music in both *Seven Samurai* and *Yojimbo* has had an influence on other film makers and film music composers – not least Sergio Leone and Ennio Morricone. The music in *Seven Samurai* was composed by Kurosawa's longstanding colleague Fumio Hayasaka who died before the completion of Kurosawa's next film, to be replaced by his pupil Sato Masaru. The working relationship with Hayasaka was important to Kurosawa: 'Working with Hayasaka, I began to think in terms of the counterpoint of sound and image as opposed to the union of sound and image' (Kurosawa, 1983).

This idea of counterpoint is perhaps not so evident in *Seven Samurai* as in other films that Kurosawa himself cites, although there is a striking use of ominous music at the beginning of the film as the farmers go towards the mill to consult Gisaku. He is offering them advice and hope, but the music suggests danger. Later the mill will be burnt by the bandits, but at this stage we don't know that. Inside the mill, the rhythmic 'clunk' of the water wheel provides another seemingly ominous background sound.

the wind beating against the banner

The use of music and sound in *Seven Samurai* is complex and there are several different musical elements featuring different styles and instrumentation. Richie (1996) suggests that the samurai and the farmers have different themes, and Kemp (2000) suggests that there are different 'leitmotifs' for each set of characters. Kikuchiyo certainly attracts jaunty music appropriate to his personality and function in the text (and this is often accompanied by extravagant grunts, whoops, laughs and hisses from Mifune). Kikuchiyo's 'theme' is similar in style to the striking score composed for *Yojimbo*. The young lovers also attract music that supports the more lyrical photography of their meetings in the woods. The harvesting of the barley and the planting of the rice are accompanied by rhythmic work songs with flute and hand drum (with the instruments visible in the planting scene). During the battle scenes there are drumbeats, mixed very low and accompanied by the cries of the men, the drumming of horses hooves and the sounds of wind and rain. Horns are used to inspire or to refer to the samurai code – after the funeral of Heihachi, Kikuchiyo rushes to put up the banner on top of a hut and the fanfare of horns plays out against the wind beating against the banner. This scene strongly invokes Ford's cavalry films, both in the funeral itself and the use of the banner.

The horns are one example of the different ways in which the main 'samurai' theme is used throughout the film. First introduced as the farmers search for samurai in the town, this is a motif played on brass and strings. In its 'standard' form it is strong and perhaps a little arrogant, matching the social status of the samurai in the countryside. It becomes associated mainly with Kanbei, and the 'battle' between this theme and that of Kikuchiyo is played out on the soundtrack when Kanbei responds to Kikuchiyo's request/demand to join the group. When Kanbei is attempting to recruit other samurai, his theme becomes slow and mournful when samurai refuse and higher pitched and lighter when Gorobei and Heihachi are involved. The horns represent the yearning, inspiring version of this theme, but they also seem to act as a sign of hope and optimism as against the low murmuring/humming that signals the traditional plight of the farmers (the murmurs of ancestral voices?). The music doesn't run throughout the film – there are long passages of silence or natural sounds,

dramatic use of the children's voices

such as water and Kurosawa also makes good dramatic use of the children's voices and the alarm gong struck by Kikuchiyo.

Some critics have complained that Kurosawa did not take enough care of the sound quality in *Seven Samurai*, quoting occasions when dialogue was difficult to discern. This is not so much an issue for non-Japanese-speaking audiences but it has persisted as a view until recently when Yoshimoto quotes the 'sound theorist' Michel Chion citing Kurosawa as one of the few directors to recognise quickly the potential of the new Dolby sound systems in the 1980s. This suggests that on *Seven Samurai*, Kurosawa suffered from the poor quality and limited potential of 1950s audio technology in Japan that did not match his creative ideas (effective use of sound was a lesson he learned from his mentor Yamamoto).

contexts

japanese history & culture

Japanese culture is not widely studied in the UK and even in the US there is less understanding than might be expected about Japanese history, social traditions and aesthetics. Film studies have suffered from this general ignorance so that, apart from a handful of specialists, many scholars and critics preface their work on specific Japanese films with a disclaimer about their limited experience of Japanese culture. This means that the handful of Japanese films released in Europe and North America tend not to be discussed in terms of their reception in Japan or relevance to contemporary Japanese culture.

In this chapter we shall place *Seven Samurai* in context by sketching in some of the social history of sixteenth-century Japan, in which the film is set and also the 'cultural context' of the early 1950s when it was produced. First, however, it is necessary to outline some of the major events in Japanese history as background.

MAJOR EVENTS

Japan is an island nation which has a direct relationship with a number of continental neighbours. Just as the nations of the British Isles have developed a relationship with mainland Europe over 1,000 years, so has Japan developed a relationship with its three closest neighbours, China, Korea and Russia. Like the English, the Japanese originally came from the continental mainland, displacing the local people, who remain a minority in contemporary Japan.

Again like the English, the Japanese enjoyed a long period without foreign invasion. In the thirteenth century, Japan was under attack by the Mongols

SEVEN SAMURAI

history & culture

who had swept across the whole of Asia, but their large invasion fleet was suddenly blown off course by a 'divine wind' (the *kamikaze* – the name given to suicide bombers at the end of the Second World War) and Japan was saved. In the first millennium AD, the Japanese borrowed ideas about government from China and the country came to be ruled by a 'divine' being – the Emperor – who was never seen by ordinary people and who stayed in his palace in Nara and later Kyoto. From the twelfth century onwards, the Emperor's power was largely usurped by noble families or 'clans' who directly controlled large areas of land. Different clans then claimed supreme power for a period in the form of a shogunate – a military dictatorship.

By the sixteenth century the balance of power amongst the noble families had been disrupted and the nobles began to act as warlords and to fight amongst themselves about who should control the country. Also at this time various European explorers, missionaries and traders began to try to 'open up' Japan to contact with the west.

In 1600, one clan – the **Tokugawas** – finally triumphed and the civil war ended (the history of the battles which led up to this point are recounted in Kurosawa's 1980 film, *Kagemusha*). The Tokugawa family held power for the next 250 years and effectively 'closed' Japan to the west. In the period when Europe and then North America experienced industrial revolution and massive social changes, Japan remained a feudal society, developing slowly but with the potential to 'leap forward' from a period of social stability. The arrival of the American Commander Perry's steamships in Tokyo harbour in 1853 is usually taken as marking the end of this long period of isolation.

The noble families were caught in a paradox. They did not want to see Japan being treated as an exploitable market by European and American traders, as China had been since the Opium Wars of the 1840s. They realised that unless there was some kind of revolutionary change in Japanese society, the country would not be strong enough to resist. But the only way change could come was through contact with the west. The result was another period of civil war that ended with the restoration of the Emperor in 1868 and the beginning of the **Meiji era.** The third quarter of the nineteenth century saw a period of unprecedented economic growth and industrial development so that, at the start of the twentieth

shock and shame of Occupation

century, Japan was able to wage war successfully against both Russia and China and to gain a foothold on the Asian mainland.

Japan eventually joined the winning side in the First World War and by the 1920s was being accepted as one of the 'Great Powers', primarily on the basis of a large modern navy. In 1926 a new Emperor began his reign as a boy (the **Showa era**) and a group of military adventurers gained control over the government. During the 1930s, Japan acted extremely aggressively against Korea and China, establishing an overseas colony in Northern China (Manchuria/Manchuko) and in Korea. Full-scale war with China was engineered in 1937 and in 1941 Japan attacked American and British bases in East Asia. At the height of her military success, Japan occupied most of East Asia and much of the Pacific. But Japanese economic performance was unable to match that of the Americans and the lines of communication between the 'home islands' and the front line were not well enough established to sustain the war effort. Defeat was inevitable and, when it came in 1945, the Japanese economy and much of Japanese social life were almost completely destroyed. The war ended soon after the Americans dropped atomic bombs on Hiroshima and Nagasaki, but even without these terrible events Japan would have been forced to surrender.

In 1945, Japan was still ruled by an 'unseen' Emperor and despite the industrial development and sophisticated urban life of a large section of the population, Japan was not a democracy – not a 'modern state' as understood in the west. America occupied Japan for the next six and a half years and in that time General McArthur, the American commanding general and effective ruler of the country, forced through constitutional changes. The shock and shame of Occupation was great and 1945 is as important a date as 1600 and 1868 in marking a major change in the lives of Japanese people. *Seven Samurai* was produced just eight years later.

SAMURAI & SIXTEENTH-CENTURY SOCIETY

> Samurai means, literally, 'those who serve', implying the rendering of honourable military service by an élite to an overlord ... three factors – military prowess, élitism and service to another – are the keys to identifying the origin of the samurai.
>
> *Turnbull, 1996, p. 9*

cinema in japan

This useful definition goes some way to explaining some of the expectations of the characters in *Seven Samurai*. Japan in the sixteenth century had a strictly defined caste system. At the top was the Emperor and the Imperial family – although he did not wield political power, the Emperor's divine right to be recognised as superior remained. The effective rulers, whose squabbles in this period led to the civil war, were the major landowners, the *daimyo*. The *daimyo* were in effect 'superior samurai' who had used their status and military prowess to gather power. They in turn 'retained' other samurai to act as their generals, leading armies of foot soldiers. The other distinct groups in society were the monks and priests (Japan has long had Buddhist as well as Shinto priests), the peasant farmers and the artisans and merchants in towns. Beneath all of these were common labourers and beggars.

The samurai retained by the 'lords' were a highly privileged group, brought up to follow not only a warrior's life, learning all the skills of war, but also the cultivation of art and poetry and music. Samurai were 'rounded', cultured individuals, expected to appreciate fine pottery as well as being able to lop off an opponent's head with precision. Such warriors would expect to marry within their own class and would be feared by the other classes.

A samurai warrior who lost his patron, perhaps when his lord was defeated in battle or disgraced, would become a 'masterless samurai', a **ronin**. At various times and especially in the civil war periods, there were many *ronin* on the highways of Japan, looking for 'honourable' employment. Such are the 'hungry samurai' of *Seven Samurai*. The narrative of *Seven Samurai* at first sight seems contrived, but the story was developed after considerable research by Kurosawa into how samurai lived in the sixteenth century – what they ate, how they dressed and the details of their daily routine.

cinema in japan

The cinema was one of the western influences on Japan towards the end of the 'modernising' Meiji era. Japanese entrepreneurs were quick to develop specifically Japanese films based on existing forms of theatre, and the first major Japanese studio, Nikkatsu, was established in 1912, before *jidaigeki* and *gendaigeki*

the consolidation in Hollywood. Shochiku followed in 1920 and by the late 1920s the Japanese film industry was putting out more films than anywhere else in the world (600–800) as well as importing the American and European films seen by Kurosawa (see Thompson & Bordwell, 1994).

The Japanese studios were, like Hollywood, vertically integrated – the same companies produced, distributed and exhibited films. During the 1930s most studios followed a policy of organising production so that their exhibition chains could receive a double bill each week. This would usually comprise a 'period' film, a *jidaigeki* and a 'modern film', a *gendaigeki*. These were the two 'mega genres' of Japanese Cinema. The former would be produced in Kyoto, 'traditional' capital of Japan, and the latter in Tokyo, the 'modern' capital. In order to appeal as widely as possible, one of the two films would appeal to women and one to men.

Jidaigeki developed from early film versions of traditional **Kabuki theatre** and tended towards highly stylised action pictures with choreographed fight scenes. (Kabuki was a popular form and still the dominant form of live entertainment. Live shows lasted for up to five hours. As a consequence, film shows were also long – *Seven Samurai* was not a particularly long film by Japanese standards.) *Gendaigeki* also developed from earlier forms, based on **shinpa theatre** – the modern drama style developed on western theatre lines at the end of the nineteenth century – and were typically melodramas or romances. It wasn't until the 1920s that women were generally allowed to appear on screen (male impersonators had been used previously) and a 'modern' cinema was properly established, but the visual style of many of the films was advanced and complex. Yoshimoto (2000) suggests that the establishment of a balance between *jidaigeki* and *gendaigeki* was essential to the formation of modern Japan – the contrast between the two made audiences more aware of the representation of ideas, of the sense that the society was being 'made modern'.

DEVELOPMENT OF *JIDAIGEKI*

Some discussion of the *jidaigeki* is necessary in order to appreciate the innovations in Kurosawa's work on *Seven Samurai*. Yoshimoto gives a detailed account of the development of the genre as part of his study of

cinema in japan

the film. He suggests that one of the reasons for its popularity in the 1920s and 1930s (when stars of **chanbara** – swordfight films – became major figures) was the popularity of new magazines offering popular literature, **taishu bungaku**. These 'one yen' books had an impact rather like the 'pulp fiction' of Hollywood and although they covered several genres of popular fiction, *chanbara* was the main form. The books and the films had what today would be termed a symbiotic relationship, feeding off the popularity of each other. At the same time a new form of theatre also helped to develop more realistic choreography of the swordfight and this moved into the *jidaigeki*, replacing the slower and more stylised movements derived from Kabuki. With this popularity and a much slicker production adding to the narrative drive, *jidaigeki* could compete with American films in the Japanese market.

Jidaigeki didn't refer to just any period. In the main they were concerned with the Tokugawa or Edo era, the long years of relative stability up to the mid nineteenth century, that nevertheless were developing the preconditions for modernisation. Yoshimoto goes to some length to stress that the *jidaigeki* set in the Edo era were not films of nostalgia for a traditional Japan. The period was presented in an idealised way and Yoshimoto argues that the setting allowed film makers to show spectacle as expected by modern audiences, but not realisable in depictions of contemporary Japan. *Jidaigeki*, although set in the past, were in fact about the present. They were a way of representing a rebellion against the traditions of Kabuki and, by assimilating ideas from American films, film makers were able to produce a 'modern' Japanese form that could carry political comments about the present. In the late 1920s *jidaigeki* were often associated with young radicals and leftists.

From this analysis of *jidaigeki*, it isn't difficult to see the possibility that the role of these films in Japanese society was not unlike the role of the Western in Hollywood at various periods, but especially in the 1950s–70s, when Hollywood would comment on current events (e.g. civil rights, Vietnam etc.) by constructing similar narratives set in the period of the Western frontier (roughly 1865–95).

cinema in japan

attacked by the military authorities

JIDAIGEKI IN THE 1950S

Cinema was one of the chief concerns of the Occupation authorities in the immediate aftermath of the war in 1945. They believed that it was supremely important to change the attitudes of the Japanese population towards military prowess and that it was dangerous to allow the production of *jidaigeki*. The Americans saw such films as validating the military code of **Bushido** and the feudalistic sentiment that had supported the aggressive expansionism of Japan in the 1930s. Such films would remind audiences of the recent past when the divinity of the Emperor was more important than concepts of democratic government and moral responsibility.

Yoshimoto argues that the Occupation authorities misunderstood both *jidaigeki* and the Kabuki theatre that had been its original model. They moved to accept Kabuki as a stylised traditional form, devoid of political meaning, but maintained a ban on *jidaigeki*, especially if films contained swordplay. Thus *jidaigeki* were both attacked by the military authorities in the 1930s as 'radical' and by the Americans in 1945 as 'feudalistic'.

Strict censorship ended in 1949 but the Japanese censors who replaced the Americans, and the film industry itself, held back from promoting a revival of *jidaigeki* and in 1950 there were only a handful produced, including Kurosawa's *Rashomon*. Very quickly, however, the genre re-established itself and by 1952 as many as ninety *jidaigeki* were released. Yoshimoto suggests that the new wave of productions, especially at the Toei studio, were characterised by a return to stylised rather than realistic swordplay and, in their avoidance of sexually explicit material, were relatively 'wholesome' fare.

KUROSAWA & *JIDAIGEKI*

Kurosawa worked for Toho, one of the major studios, and his first film *Sanshiro Sugata* (1943) was a *jidaigeki* about a judo student. It was unusual in replacing the typical swordfight with a series of unarmed combats. A routine sequel was made by Kurosawa, at the studio's insistence, in 1945. Before the war ended he produced a short historical feature based on a Kabuki story, but this was unreleased until 1952. Otherwise, before *Rashomon*, he worked on contemporary films, some dealing with the

cinema in japan

social issues of the Occupation. His next two films before *Seven Samurai* also had contemporary settings. Dower (1999) reports that Kurosawa's wartime films were ordered to be destroyed by the Occupation authorities, but that he soon adjusted to a new set of censors after a similar experience with the wartime military authorities.

Rashomon is remembered because of its intriguing narrative structure – four versions of the same event seen from the perspective of different characters. This film did have a connection with contemporary society in its fairly abstract references to what humans do at times of chaos and social unrest, but its historical setting did not raise significant questions about the development of *jidaigeki*. *Seven Samurai*, by contrast, was a conscious attempt to make a new kind of *jidaigeki*.

Whereas the conventional *jidaigeki* offered an idealised view of the Edo period, Kurosawa set out to make a 'realistic' film about samurai life in the civil war period of the sixteenth century. This doesn't mean that he set out to make an historically accurate representation of events. The story of *Seven Samurai* was an original fiction but, unlike in the conventional *jidaigeki*, Kurosawa dressed his actors and sets according to old paintings and historical descriptions. All the film's main characters were given full motivations and subplots to enable their actions to be placed in context. So, for instance, the film shows the farmers training in how to defend their village. They wield whatever weapons are to hand. Rather than depict choreographed swordfights with conventional moves, Kurosawa story-boarded more realistic fights in which characters defended or attacked in any way they could given their circumstances.

Seven Samurai was exceptional in the flood of *jidaigeki* that appeared in 1954. Primarily because of its careful preparation and location shooting, the film took nearly a year to complete from the start of shooting, and its budget of 210 million yen was seven times that of the average *jidaigeki*. Kurosawa was fortunate that Toho (the studio to which he had returned after several years' working on individual productions at other studios) was not a big *jidaigeki* producer and were prepared to try something different. Toei did not follow Kurosawa's example – but in the early 1960s, Kurosawa's two famous *jidaigeki*, *Yojimbo* and *Sanjuro*, did outstrip Toei's conventional offerings.

cultural context – 1954

The Occupation ended in 1952, but the changes in Japanese society that had been forced upon the country were still working their way through. The Japanese population was slowly coming to terms with ideas about personal responsibility. It was being asked to take part in a true representative democracy after experiencing a military dictatorship. It had effectively lost the security of a traditional belief in the divinity of the Emperor (or at least the 'spiritual leadership' he represented). It had to face the reality of military defeat and also face the charges that its military forces had committed terrible atrocities in the name of Imperial Japan.

The economy, shattered in 1945, had to be reconstituted and large swathes of urban Japan literally rebuilt after fire bombing and the atom bombs on Hiroshima and Nagasaki. Factories that had produced weapons had to be rebuilt for peaceful purposes. The Japanese military could be reconstituted only as a 'defence force' monitored by the Americans.

Dower asserts that there was no single 'Japanese' response to all these problems (even if the Occupation authorities tended to think that there was a distinct 'Japanese personality').

> No-one on either side, however, predicted how diverse and spirited would be the response to defeat – and to liberation from war and wartime regimentation. Because the defeat was so shattering, the surrender so unconditional, the disgrace of the militarists so complete, the misery the 'holy war' had brought home so personal, starting over involved not merely reconstructing buildings but also rethinking what it meant to speak of a good life and good society
> *(Dower, 1999, p. 25).*

The 'diverse responses' ranged from those who wished for a return to the premilitary society to those who embraced American consumerism as quickly as possible. It was difficult to find new leaders and people to fill positions of responsibility – sometimes the same people who had been in power before the war emerged in different guises. Dower suggests that

SEVEN SAMURAI

readings

Kurosawa's contemporary films (*gendaigeki*) picked up on this, by presenting 'a generally humanistic [male] individual who was sometimes cursed by the past and almost always found himself mired in a venal, duplicitous society. In film after film, this protagonist, invariably played by Toshiro Mifune, moved through an increasingly dismal milieu of gangsters, ex-soldiers turned criminals, venal journalists and helpless, deranged innocents' (p. 427).

It is not difficult to see the appearance of *Seven Samurai* in 1954 as a positive and optimistic response to the end of this period. Faced with the chaos of the sixteenth-century civil war, the farmers organise themselves and make arrangements with the samurai to protect their village. The samurai provide leadership and training and encourage collective effort, recognising the importance of individual contributions. The farmers and samurai recognise their differences and, for the moment, agree to co-operate. They defeat the bandits, the representatives of chaos, and the farmers are able to return to their function of planting and harvesting – an activity essential for the well being of everyone.

readings of seven samurai in cultural context

Yoshimoto suggests that much of the critical writing about *Seven Samurai* adopts the approach of looking for an **allegorical** reading. These readings are as diverse as the responses to defeat suggested by Dower above. Sato Tadao suggests that the film might be seen as a justification for the 1954 formation of the National Self-Defence Force (which was technically a breach of the 1947 Constitution). A newspaper review saw the images of the dead samurai as offering a commemoration of the Japanese killed in the Second World War. Others suggested that the film was an analysis of class struggle and of the place of individual heroism or intellectual work within a community seeking to create a civil society.

'the triumph of the human spirit'

Perhaps the pithiest comment came from Masayoshi Iwabutchi writing on the Japanese film year of 1954 for *Sight and Sound* in 1955: 'Some critics attacked the film but failed to understand its important message; the implication throughout this story ... is that unity is necessary for any kind of progress.' This article is also useful in pointing to the 373 films produced in Japan in 1954. Amongst these was a wide variety of *gendaigeki*, including several other 'humanist' films as well as documentaries. But there were also 'militarist' and 'antimilitarist' films that directly intervened in the national debate about rearmament. Few of these films reached the west and only a handful such as Mizoguchi's *Chickamatsu Monogatari* (a *jidaigeki*) have remained in circulation. It is therefore very difficult to place *Seven Samurai* in context with confidence – inevitably attention has focused on the enduring qualities of the film more than its direct links to events in 1953/4.

HUMANISM

Most writers about *Seven Samurai* focus on one aspect of the film's ideology above all others – the 'humanism' evident in the film, as it is in most of Kurosawa's work. Humanism in relation to film theory or critical writing is very much a phenomenon of the period from the end of the Second World War through the 1950s and up to the **French New Wave** and the triumph of modernism. What does it mean? *Chambers 20th Century Dictionary* refers to 'literary culture [as distinct from religious texts], any system which puts human interests and the mind of man paramount, rejecting the supernatural'. Writing at the end of a period when one long struggle against Fascism had come to an end, but a cold war between capitalism and Communism had just begun, critics were particularly responsive towards films that turned away from the great power struggles and instead concentrated on social issues and stories about 'the triumph of the human spirit'.

Critics in the US, UK and other parts of Europe tended to respond to the same films, many of which circulated via the major festivals at Venice and Cannes. The critical orthodoxy in the late 1940s and early 1950s was in favour of Italian **neo-realism** and other 'realist' cinemas that used location filming and explored social issues. It is certainly the case that some of Kurosawa's *gendaigeki* dealt directly with the social issues in demonstrating human weaknesses

contemporary Japan and in all his films there is an interest in minor characters and the variety of human experience. But Kurosawa's humanism in *Seven Samurai* is not the same as the 'liberal humanism' of European critics. It is more a recognition of the harshness of life in the sixteenth century and the acceptance that people will act like human beings, motivated by basic desires and demonstrating human weaknesses. In *Seven Samurai*, the samurai themselves and the **Bushido** code are faced with human emotions that are not compatible with honourable behaviour. Take the case of the old woman who wants to die because she has no family left after the bandits killed her son. Heihachi tries to cheer her up but Kikuchiyo says he cannot bear her misery (an honest response at least). Later when Kuzeo and Katsushiro capture a bandit for interrogation, Kanbei stops the villagers from killing the prisoner on the grounds that he has given information – he is a prisoner of war. But Kanbei is powerless to stop the old woman who staggers into view wielding a harrow with the intention of avenging her son. 'Help her!' cries the old man Gisaku and Kanbei turns away – he cannot go against her desire for vengeance.

Bert Cardullo as quoted in Perry (1997) gives this account of human action in the film:

> *Seven Samurai* is a film about circumstance, or about man and his relationship, at his best, to circumstance; it is not a film about fate. In tragedy, man acts, often stupidly if inevitably, and then reflects on his actions, wisely. In the work of circumstance, man acts wisely in the face of the stupidity and unpredictability of circumstance ... [it is] real or tangible; man is most often defeated by it. At his best, he meets it (the adverse kind, that is) on equal ground, and if he does not triumph, he does not lose, either. He distinguishes himself in the fight. That is all, and that is enough.
>
> Bert Cardullo, 'The Circumstance of the East, the Fate of the West,'
> Literature/Film Quarterly, vol. 13, no. 2 (1985), p. 112-17.

There is nothing sentimental about *Seven Samurai*. When Kanbei says he will punish anyone who deserts his post, we know he means it. It's worth noting too that *Seven Samurai* was awarded the relatively new 'X' certificate on its 1955 release in the UK – British censors thought it was too strong for audiences under sixteen. But despite the coldness in direction detected by 'GL' (probably Gavin Lambert), the *Monthly Film Bulletin* reviewer in 1955, there is a rational, 'human' core to the film. Philip Kemp in his commentary on the film points to the pragmatism of Kanbei and the samurai he recruits. When he meets his old friend Schichiroji, he asks him how he escaped from a battle – 'I hid in a ditch'. Heihachi, when asked how he responds when there are too many of the enemy to kill, says that he runs away. These are rational responses and Kemp makes the point that they are not like the warriors who would fight to the death simply because the code demands it – as it had for too many soldiers in the Second World War.

seven samurai's influence on film makers

In this section reference is made to well known cases of the direct influence of *Seven Samurai* and Kurosawa's work generally on international film makers. Much of the influence on film making generally is not recorded because it manifests itself in terms of dozens of film makers 'trying out' new ways to shoot a particular scene. Kurosawa's great strength as a craftsman was his ability to deploy such a wide range of camera techniques. He was not necessarily the first director to use a particular technique but he combined relatively new or under-used techniques in new ways.

Three specific techniques stand out – shooting action scenes with **multiple cameras**, using **telephoto** lenses to 'plunge into the mêlée' of the fight and **overcranking** the camera to produce slow motion in the projected image. (See Style for detailed descriptions.) The combination of these three techniques meant that the battles in *Seven Samurai* looked very different from what had gone before. It is safe to assume that wherever *Seven Samurai* was shown in the mid 1950s, directors, cinematographers and putative film makers were wondering 'how did he do that?' and then going away with plans to try to find out.

This was certainly true of theatre and television director Sam Peckinpah was one of Kurosawa's biggest American fans in the 1950s, first because of *Rashomon* and then *Seven Samurai*. Peckinpah had spent time as a young man in Mexico and as a marine in China, overseeing the Japanese withdrawal. He recognised the truthfulness of Kurosawa's depiction of village life and there is an obvious debt to *Seven Samurai* in the plot development of *The Wild Bunch* (1969) in which a gang of American 'outlaws' cross over into Mexico in 1911 escaping the 'end of the Western frontier' by becoming embroiled in the Mexican revolution. The film ends with the Bunch effectively sacrificing themselves in a futile attempt to save one of their number – a young Mexican villager. But it wasn't just a narrative idea that Peckinpah borrowed. He was fascinated by Kurosawa's technique in filming the action scenes and particularly the final battle – the use of slow motion through 'over-cranking' and the deployment of three or more cameras to film simultaneously.

Peckinpah had attempted to develop Kurosawa's ideas in *Major Dundee* (1965) (a film cut against Peckinpah's wishes), but finally achieved what he wanted in *The Wild Bunch*. The latter film has itself been widely imitated, being released at the high point of American involvement in Vietnam and signalling a change in the representation of violence on screen. It is fair to say that Kurosawa's handling of battle scenes changed the representation of combat on the screen. Here is Zhang Yimou, one of the leading directors (although trained as a cinematographer) of contemporary Chinese cinema:

> As a cinematographer, I am awed by Kurosawa's filming of grand spectacle, particularly battle scenes. Even today I cannot figure out his method. I checked our film library and found that he used only 200 or so horses for certain battle scenes that suggest thousands. Other film makers have more money, more advanced techniques, more special effects. Yet no one has surpassed him.
>
> *Zhang Yimou, Asia Now (Time Magazine) August 1990, vol 154, nos 7/8*

Yimou is clearly referring to later films such as *Kagemusha*, but there is little doubt that his remarks can also be applied to *Seven Samurai*.

influence on film makers contexts

slowed down by dialogue

The most obvious tribute to *Seven Samurai* from Hollywood came with the remake directed by John Sturges in 1960. This was a tribute in the sense that Hollywood recognised the storytelling power of the film – otherwise the remake as *The Magnificent Seven* showed little interest in the complexity of the Japanese original. Joseph L. Anderson's 1962 comparison of the two films begins with the observation that the remake 'reveals some of the fixed ideas that inhibit American film making'. Anderson's paper is particularly useful because it was written soon after the American re-make was released, at a time when international interest in Kurosawa was reaching a peak.

Anderson suggests two main ways in which Sturges was frustrated in his attempts to match Kurosawa's achievement. First, the Hollywood version is slowed down by dialogue. All the characters are required to explain themselves and to justify what they do, so that the moral message of the film comes across. The overall effect is to simplify the complexities of the narrative so that it becomes a 'good v. evil' tale and individual characters become simply 'types', representing different aspects of each side. (Kurosawa's characters are also types to some extent, but they also have sufficient individuality to suggest a real community with relationships between themselves.) Second, Sturges does attempt to recreate something of Kurosawa's visual style, albeit within the much wider CinemaScope frame. Anderson praises Sturges for 'liberating' the Scope camera in allowing it to track, but notes that otherwise he is unable to match both Kurosawa's deep understanding of landscape and environment (the wind and rain) as setting, and his mastery of a wide range of techniques, enabling the presentation of dramatic action. In short, Kurosawa's characters act rather than speak and the cinematography represents their movement rather than simply photographing them.

Anderson concludes with a section arguing for Kurosawa's status as auteur (in 1962 a relatively new concept in the US). He points to the development of Kurosawa's use of the camera and editing over a series of films and to the figure of Kanbei as an almost autobiographical creation. However, it is not only personal style and vision, but also his status vis-à-vis the studio that enable Kurosawa to achieve what he wants in the film. Sturges by contrast 'is only the most important talent on a work which

SEVEN SAMURAI

has been shaped by many men, and compromised by many Hollywood conventions'. *The Magnificent Seven* demonstrates Kurosawa's importance by what it fails to do. With Kurosawa's hero John Ford close to the end of his distinguished career, this failure (in artistic terms – *The Magnificent Seven* was a box-office smash hit, most of all in Japan and Europe) emphasised that if the American Western was going to change, it was going to need an auteur figure prepared to take on the studios. Arguably, Peckinpah, just beginning his film career after a decade in television, was the director who followed Kurosawa's model (see Weddle, 1996) for extensive accounts of Peckinpah's struggle to complete *The Wild Bunch*)

Anderson's final comment announces that a minor United Artists producer was considering a Western based on Kurosawa's then current release, *Yojimbo* (1962) starring Toshiro Mifune as a **ronin**. That film never appeared as a recognisable re-make, but several years later United Artists did release an Italian re-make of *Yojimbo*, starring a young American television cowboy, Clint Eastwood. *A Fistful of Dollars* (Italy, 1964) represented a re-make of Kurosawa that was much more self-conscious about 'borrowing'. Christopher Frayling (1981 and 1999) gives a detailed account of the production of *A Fistful of Dollars* and how writer/director Sergio Leone created a 'new' Western which challenged Hollywood conventions. Leone's approach differed significantly from Kurosawa's but was equally striking. Frayling offers no direct evidence that Leone was particularly inspired by *Seven Samurai*, although there is little doubt that he would have seen the film, but he was certainly an admirer of *The Magnificent Seven* which was popular in Italy.

Even if there is no direct link between Leone and *Seven Samurai*, it is worth pointing to the reverence both Kurosawa and Leone showed towards John Ford and the impact both had upon the future of the American Western. Leone borrowed certain ideas from Kurosawa, including the mélange of music and sounds on the soundtrack of *A Fistful of Dollars*, the low and high camera angles and the dramatic switches from long shot to big close-up that became a trademark of the Western trilogy (i.e. including *For a Few Dollars More* and *The Good, The Bad and The Ugly*). He also took something from the amorality of Kurosawa's *jidaigeki*. Otherwise, there are big differences in theme. The issue of a 'community', like the village in

spoofing a Kurosawa-inspired film

Seven Samurai, doesn't appear in the trilogy and Leone is not so interested in the relationship between the individual and the group. Nevertheless, it could be argued that the joint assault upon the American Western brought about by the international success of *Seven Samurai* and later *A Fistful of Dollars* both revitalised a major American genre and established the importance of the international cinema market and international cinema production in the eyes of traditionally insular Hollywood producers.

As a final tribute to the storytelling power of *Seven Samurai*, the independent Hollywood producer Roger Corman brought out a 1980 spoof of *Star Wars* entitled *Battle Beyond the Stars* in which seven intergalactic heroes defend a lonely planet from attack by a warlord. With a plot borrowed entirely from *The Magnificent Seven* this meant a Kurosawa-derived script spoofing a Kurosawa-inspired film.

SEVEN SAMURAI & THE INTERNATIONAL FILM INDUSTRY

The detailed statistical information about international box office that is available today via trade magazines such as *Screen International* was not presented for publication in the 1950s and is not easily accessible. All that can be said with certainty is that the film was very expensive (see above), that it was 'popular', but not massively so, in Japan and that it was successfully released around the world. Its current status as a cinema classic can be judged by the recent re-releases of the film on video, laser disc and most recently DVD. Up until the demise of the so-called 'arthouse repertory' sector of UK cinemas in the 1980s, *Seven Samurai* was regularly revived.

This longevity and classic status has not been without struggle. Long films (i.e. three hours or more) have had a chequered history in US and UK distribution. Sometimes they are in fashion, but much of the time they are not. Cinemas want to sell tickets and long films mean less showings each day and the prospect of less revenue. *Seven Samurai* was originally released in Japan at 207 minutes. It first appeared on international release in a shorter version (155 minutes in the UK, 169 mins in the US) and was cut again at different times and in different territories. The current DVD

production & reception

version in the UK, used in this Note, runs to 190 minutes, the equivalent of around 198 minutes at film speed, so there are still a few minutes missing.

production & reception

Film studies now require consideration of production history and audience reception of specific titles, but little is known about the original release of *Seven Samurai* in 1954. Although it was at the time the most expensive film ever made in Japan, Kurosawa always complained that the Japanese industry wanted to make films cheaply. He was quite prepared to sit out the long periods during production when the money ran out, confident that as long as his films were successful at the box office, Toho would eventually find the extra money to complete his film, and throughout the 1950s this proved to be the case.

About its reception all that can be said with confidence is that it made money in Japan and that critics at home didn't like it as much as (most) critics abroad. Now that it has achieved classic status, there are plenty of contemporary viewers who will attest to its status as action film and character-based story.

CRITICS ON *SEVEN SAMURAI*

No mention has yet been made of gender or sexuality. *Seven Samurai* conforms to a traditional view of action films that sees them as primarily male texts. There are few significant roles for women – the old woman who has lost her son, Shino the peasant's daughter and Rikichi's wife, abducted by the bandits. The young women of the village are kept mainly out of sight and out of the samurai's reach. The film (and Kurosawa's work in general) has tended to be ignored by feminist criticism. But there are readings that refer to the homoeroticism of aspects of the film:

> The homoerotic undertones, inevitable in such a masculine world, ripple through the story and add weight to it. The young samurai's devotion to both Kanbei and Kyuzo skirts the masochistic, as he repeatedly kneels before both in praise and supplication. Kurosawa is well aware of this, as he focuses repeatedly on the boy's intense,

production & reception contexts

'the most tender-hearted of great film makers'

transported smile and burning eyes. Mifune, always praised as an actor but vastly underrated as a hunk, is a vision of butch bravado. In one scene, he entertains his fellow samurai by stripping to a g-string to catch a fish. In the whole last sequence, he wears a sort of abbreviated chain mail vest that shows his smooth muscular arms and exposed ass – one of cinema's finest – to great advantage.

Gary Morris, in Bright Lights Film Journal, 1996

The 'masculine' tone of the film may also account for references to Kurosawa's work that compare it unfavourably to that of Mizoguchi. This is particularly the case of the critics of *Cahiers du cinéma* who in the 1950s seemed unable to accept both the Japanese directors who won prizes at Venice. In his usual extravagant way, Jean-Luc Godard could only praise Mizoguchi by putting down Kurosawa. It is unfortunate perhaps, but Kurosawa's work has often been placed in a specific context not of his own choosing. So for those critics (like Godard) who prefer melodrama and mise-en-scène to action and editing, it is viewed as inferior to Mizoguchi. To a critic like Noël Burch the work must be subsumed within an argument about the legacy of Eisenstein's editing technique and for a range of critics in the 1950s (liberals in England, some of the *Cahiers* group in Paris, Japanese critics) the context is a positive or negative 'exoticism' or a narrowly defined humanism.

Perhaps only now, nearly fifty years after its initial release, can *Seven Samurai* be viewed objectively, the 'illusion' peeled away to reveal the 'reality', as in Michael Wilmington's obituary tribute to Kurosawa:

At his greatest, he gives us the exhilaration of battle, but also its tragedy, absurdity and sorrow. That double vision is the secret of his art. Beneath the brutality he was one of the most tender-hearted of great film makers.

Wilmington, 1999

bibliography

general film

Altman, Rick, *Film Genre*, BFI, 1999
 Detailed exploration of the concept of film genre

Bordwell, David, *Narration in the Fiction Film*, Routledge, 1985
 A detailed study of narrative theory and structures

– – –, Staiger, Janet & Thompson, Kristin, *The Classical Hollywood Cinema: Film Style & Mode of Production to 1960*, Routledge, 1985; pbk 1995
 An authoritative study of cinema as institution, it covers film style and production

– – – & Thompson, Kristin, *Film Art*, McGraw-Hill, 4th edn, 1993
 An introduction to film aesthetics for the non-specialist; contains an analysis of *North by Northwest*, looking closely at narrative structure and narration

Branson, Gill & Stafford, Roy, *The Media Student's Book*, Routledge, 2nd edn, 1999

Buckland, Warren, *Teach Yourself Film Studies*, Hodder & Stoughton, 1988
 Very accessible, it gives an overview of key areas in film studies

Cook, Pam & Bernink, Mieke (eds), *The Cinema Book*, BFI, 2nd edn, 1999

Corrigan, Tim, *A Short Guide To Writing About Film*, Harper Collins, 1994
 What it says: a practical guide for students

Dyer, Richard with Paul McDonald, *Stars*, BFI, 2nd edn, 1998
 A good introduction to the star system

Easthope, Antony, *Classical Film Theory*, Longman, 1993
 A clear overview of writing about film theory

Hayward, Susan, *Key Concepts in Cinema Studies*, Routledge, 1996

Hill, John & Gibson, Pamela Church (eds), *The Oxford Guide to Film Studies*, Oxford University Press, 1998
 Wide-ranging standard guide; includes a chapter by Barbara Creed that provides an overview of research and writing on film and psychoanalysis

Lapsley, Robert & Westlake, Michael, *Film Theory: An Introduction*, Manchester University Press, 1994

Maltby, Richard & Craven, Ian, *Hollywood Cinema*, Blackwell, 1995
 A comprehensive work on the Hollywood industry and its products

Mulvey, Laura, 'Visual Pleasure and Narrative Cinema' (1974), in *Visual and Other Pleasures*, Indiana University Press, Bloomington, 1989
 The classic analysis of 'the look' and 'the male gaze' in Hollywood cinema. Also available in numerous other edited collections

Nelmes, Jill (ed.), *Introduction to Film Studies*, Routledge, 2nd edn, 1999
 Deals with several national cinemas and key concepts in film study

Nowell–Smith, Geoffrey (ed.), *The Oxford History of World Cinema*, Oxford University Press, 1996
 Hugely detailed and wide-ranging with many features on 'stars'

general   bibliography

Thomson – Kitses

Thomson, David, **A Biographical Dictionary of the Cinema**, Secker & Warburg, 1975
   Unashamedly driven by personal taste, but often stimulating

Truffaut, François, **Hitchcock**, Simon & Schuster, 1966, rev. edn, Touchstone, 1985
   Landmark extended interview

Turner, Graeme, **Film as Social Practice**, 3rd edn, Routledge, 1999
   Chapter four, 'Film Narrative', discusses structuralist theories of narrative

Wollen, Peter, **Signs and Meaning in the Cinema**, BFI, 1997, rev. edn,
   An important study in semiology

Readers should also explore the many relevant websites and journals. *Film Education* and *Sight and Sound* are standard reading.

Valuable websites include:

The Internet Movie Database at www.uk.imdb.com

Screensite at www.tcf.ua.edu/screensite/contents.html

The Media and Communications Site at the University of Aberystwyth at www.aber.ac.uk/~dgc/welcome.html

There are obviously many other university and studio websites which are worth exploring in relation to film studies

seven samurai

Anderson, Joseph L., 'When the Twain Meet: Hollywood's Remake of *The Seven Samurai*', in *Film Quarterly*, vol. 15 no. 3, Spring 1962

Bock, Audie, **Japanese Film Directors**, Kodansha International, 1978

Bordwell, David & Thompson, Kristin, **Film History: An Introduction**, McGraw-Hill, 1994

Bordwell, David & Thompson, Kristin, **Film Art, An Introduction**, Knopf, 2nd Edition 1986

Burch, Noël, 'Akira Kurosawa' in Richard Roud (ed.), *Cinema: A Critical Dictionary*, Martin Secker & Warburg, 1980

Cardullo, Bert. 'The Circumstance of the East, the Fate of the West', in *Literature & Film Quarterly* vol. 13, no. 2 1985

Dower, John, **Embracing Defeat**, Penguin Press, 1999
   Excellent background to the social and political conditions in Japan from 1945–52

Ehrlich, Linda C. & Desser, David (eds), **Cinematic Landscapes: Observations on the Visual arts and Cinema of China and Japan**, University of Texas Press, 1994

Frayling, Christopher, **Spaghetti Westerns**, Routledge & Kegan Paul, 1981

Frayling, Christopher, **Sergio Leone**, Faber & Faber, 1999

Iwabutchi, Masayoshi, '1954 in Japan', in *Sight and Sound*, Spring 1955

Kemp, Philip, **Commentary on Seven Samurai**, UK DVD release, BFI, 2000

Kitses, Jim, **Horizons West**, Thames & Hudson, 1969

websites

Kurosawa, Akira, *Something Like an Autobiography*, Vintage Books, 1983

Kurosawa, Akira, Interviewed on *Arena*, BBC2, 1986

Morris, Gary, 'Seven Samurai', *Bright Lights Film Journal*, no 17, September 1996 (see www.brightlightsfilm.com/17/10_samurai.html)

Owen, David, tribute to Toshiro Mifune, programme notes for Japan Center 1984 (see http://www.sprout.org/toshiro/)

Parshall, Peter F., 'East Meets West: Casablanca vs. *The Seven Samurai*', in *Literature & Film Quarterly*, vol 17, no 4 1989

Richardson, Tony, 'The Seven Samurai', in *Sight and Sound*, vol 24, no 4, Spring 1955

Richie, Donald, 'The Influence of Traditional Aesthetics on Japanese Film', in Ehrlich & Desser (eds) *op. cit.*, 1994

Richie, Donald, *The Films of Akira Kurosawa*, University of California Press, 2nd edition 1996
    A new edition of this standard work was published in 1998.

Tadao, Sato, *Currents in Japanese Cinema*, Kodansha International, 1982

Tadao, Sato, 'Japanese Cinema and the Traditional Arts', in Ehrlich & Desser (eds), *op. cit.*, 1994

Turnbull, Stephen, *Samurai: The Warrior Tradition*, Arms and Armour Press, 1996

Weddle, David, *Sam Peckinpah: 'If They Move. . . Kill'Em!'*, Faber & Faber, 1996

Wilmington, Michael & Hogue, Peter, 'Akira Kurosawa 1910–98', in *Film Comment*, vol 35, no 1, January–February 1999

Yoshimoto, Mitsuhiro, *Kurosawa, Film Studies and Japanese Cinema*, Duke University Press, 2000
    The most recent publication to place Kurosawa's work in relation to Japanese cinema studies.

websites

All these websites were 'live' in February 2001

Bright Lights Magazine, http://www.brightlightsfilm.com/17/10_samurai.html

Japan Echo, http://www.japanecho.com/docs/html/250614.html
    Essay on Akira Kurosawa by Tadao Sato

Japanese Virtual Museum, http://jin.jcic.or.jp/museum/

Moviemaker Magazine, http://www.moviemaker.com/issues/31/crossing/31_crossing.html
    Essay on Akira Kurosawa by Carmen Ficarra

Robert Perry, http://www2.tky.3web.ne.jp/~adk/kurosawa/essay/No3_DAMNED_SAMURAI.html
    This essay is on the 'Akira Kurosawa Database', which includes other useful material

Time Magazine, http://www.time.com/time/asia/asia/magazine/1999/990823/kurosawa1.html
    Zhang Yimou's tribute to Akira Kurosawa

websites

bibliography

Toshiro Mifune – Personal homepage

Toshiro Mifune tribute, http://www. sprout.org/toshiro/

University of Adelaide, http://arts. adelaide.edu.au/person/DHart/Films/ 7Samurai.html
  Useful set of teacher/student notes

University of Arizona, http://cronkite. pp.asu.edu/jrn494/atsotsos/7sam/ maintxt.html
  A detailed essay on the social context of the film

University of Massachusetts, http:// www.enl.umassd.edu/InteractiveCourse/ EThompson/sevensamurai.html

University of Michigan, http://www. umich.edu/~iinet/cjs/films/reviews/ sevensamurai.html

Personal homepage, http://home. earthlink.net/~ronintom/Kurosawa.htm
  General Kurosawa page with links to many of the sites listed above

Personal homepage, http://www.kiwi-us. com/~watabe/samurai.html

filmography

(UK titles in brackets)

1943 *Sugata sanshiro*

1944 *Ichiban utsukushiku*
      (*The Most Beautiful*)

1945 *Tora no o wo fumu otokotachi*
      (*The Men Who Tread On the
      Tiger's Tail*)

1945 *Zoku sugata sanshiro*

1946 *Asu o tsukuru hitobito*
      (*Those Who Make Tomorrow*)

1946 *Waga seishun ni kuinashi*
      (*No Regrets for My Youth*)

1947 *Subarashiki nichiyobi*
      (*One Wonderful Sunday*)

1948 *Yoidore tenshi* (*Drunken Angel*)

1949 *Nora inu* (*Stray Dog*)

1950 *Shubun* (*Scandal*)

1950 *Rashomon*

1951 *Hakuchi* (*The Idiot*)

1952 *Ikiru* (*Living*)

1954 *Shichinin no samurai*
      (*Seven Samurai*)

1955 *Ikimono no kiroku*
      (*Record of a Living Being*)

1957 *Kumonosu jo* (*Throne of Blood*)

1957 *Donzoko* (*The Lower Depths*)

1958 *Kakushi toride no san akunin*
      (*The Hidden Fortress*)

1960 *Warui yatsu hodo yoku nemuru*
      (*The Bad Sleep Well*)

1961 *Yojimbo*

1962 *Sanjuro*

1963 *Tengoku to jigoku*
      (*High and Low*)

1965 *Akahige (Red Beard)*

1970 *Dodes'ka-den*

1974 *Dersu Uzala*

1980 *Kagemusha* (*Shadow Warrior*)

1985 *Ran* (*Chaos*)

1990 *Yume* (*Dreams*)

1991 *Hachigatsu no kyoshikyoku*
      (*Rhapsody in August*)

1993 *Madadayo*

japanese terms

benshi narrator-commentator in silent films

Bushido the feudal code of the Japanese Samurai, stressing loyalty, courage and self-discipline

chanbara sword play films

daimyo landowners who had used their status and military prowess to acquire power

emaki medieval scroll paintings that feature a narrative

gendaigeki the general term for 'contemporary' films that covers several subgenres

haiku an epigrammatic Japanese verse form consisting of seventeen syllables

Heisi era 1989 – present

ikebana Japanese decorative art of flower arranging

jidaigeki the general term for 'period' films, including *chanbara*

Kabuki theatre traditional theatre that formed the basis for early Japanese film productions, characterised by highly stylised acting and costumes with 'flat' lighting

Meiji era 1868–1912 the restoration of the Emperor and the great period of modernisation

Momoyama era 1573–1600 the main period of civil war when *Seven Samurai* and several other Kurosawa films are set

Noh theatre traditional (medieval) theatre in which actors 'must strive to exhibit on the stage the essence of a character, rather than creating any superficial outer resemblance' (Rimer)

ronin 'masterless samurai' who travelled in sixteenth century Japan, looking for work

Shinpa theatre modern drama style developed on western theatre lines at the end of the nineteenth century

Showa era 1926–1989

Taisho era 1912–1926

taishu bungaku popular one-yen literature

Tokugawa or Edo era 1600–1868 the long period of 'stability' under the Tokugawa shogunate when the capital moved to Edo (old name for Tokyo)

ukiyo-e woodblock prints from the Edo era, one of the first examples of a mass market visual text

cinematic terms

Academy ratio the universal aspect ratio of the cinema screen between 1930 and 1953 at 1.33:1

allegory a literary term: a story or situation written in such a way as to have two coherent meanings

back story an explanation of what has happened in the past and how a character finds him/herself to be in the present situation

deep focus sharp focus throughout the depth of the image – i.e. the foreground, middle ground and background are all in focus

Eisenstein, Sergei (1898–1948) Russian director active in the Soviet Union in the 1920s both as film maker and writer/theorist. Associated with ideas of editing and the representation of class struggle. Internationally famous and a major influence on world cinema

film noir French term, applied to a type of Hollywood film made in the 1940s and 1950s, characterised by low-key lighting and bleak mood, usually set in the city and featuring criminal activity

Ford, John (1894–1973) Irish-American director active from the early 1920s. Arguably the most successful American director of the classical period commercially and critically. Particularly known for directing Westerns starring John Wayne or Henry Fonda

French New Wave a movement in film in the 1950s and 1960s, notably featuring the work of François Truffaut and Jean-Luc Godard, which both celebrated Hollywood genre films in its style and broke many of the rules of continuity editing on its form of storytelling

High Concept the industry term applied to films that can be described in twenty-five words or less. It is characterised by a postmodern self-consciousness in the use of style and stars. Most blockbuster movies are constructed as High Concept films

jump cut an editing transition between two shots of similar size and subject that breaks the conventions of continuity editing and gives the effect of the image 'jumping'

Claude Lévi-Strauss French anthro-pologist whose work on myths in tribal cultures has informed film studies

mise-en-scène originally a theatre term, used by film critics in the 1950s and 1960s to refer to the work of the film director in 'staging the scene' for the camera

montage loosely used to refer to film editing, montage has two specific meanings: the principle of juxtaposing images to create new meanings, introduced in Soviet cinema in the 1920s; the use of short sequences of related images to give a quick impression of a series of events

multi-camera shooting a scene from different positions with two or more cameras simultaneously. The conventional mode in studio television production, this was unusual in the cinema in the 1950s

neo-realism approach to film production that emphasises the presentation of stories drawn from everyday life rather than 'created' by scriptwriters and uses location shooting, non-actors etc. Associated with a group of Italian film makers in the aftermath of the Second World War and widely supported by critics in the early 1950s

oppositions a critical approach to

cinematic terms

textual analysis, drawing on the work of Claude Lévi-Strauss, that searches for sets of 'binary oppositions' such as garden v. desert or freedom v. restraint. Such oppositions suggest potential narrative conflicts and themes

overcranking the practice of running film through a camera at a speed greater than 24 frames per second. When projected at the standard speed this produces 'slow motion'

pan moving the camera on its axis from side to side to produce a sweeping motion

studio system organisation of the film industry dominated by vertically integrated studios which produce, distribute and exhibit films. In Japan in the 1950s these were Toho, Nikkatsu, Shochiku, Daiei and Toei

tableau a composition in which actors are arranged as a static group (as in a painting). Associated with the work of John Ford

telephoto a 'long' lens for a camera that allows distant objects to be brought closer by distorting normal vision and removing the 'dead' ground between the viewer and the subject – not often used in 1950s' cinema

Todorov Tztevan Todorov was born in Bulgaria and contributed to the Russian Formalist school of criticism. He developed a narrative theory based on a pattern of cause and effect

tracking shot a continuous shot made with a moving camera mounted on a dolly

typage an approach to casting adopted in the 1920s by Sergei Eisenstein in which actors were chosen for their distinctive physical features, enabling easy audience recognition of character traits

wipe editing transition that literally wipes across the screen, rubbing out one image and revealing a different one. Kurosawa uses a horizontal wipe across the screen.

credits

Shichinin no samurai (1954)

UK title
Seven Samurai

US title: *The Magnificent Seven*, later *The Seven Samurai*

production company
Toho

director
Akira Kurosawa

producer
Sojiro Motogi

screenplay
Shinobu Hashimoto, Akira Kurosawa, Hideo Oguni

cinematographer
Asakazu Nakai

editors
Koichi Iwashita, Akira Kurosawa

music
Fumio Hayasaka

sound recording
Fumio Yanoguchi

production design
Takashi Matsuyama

runtime
207 minutes (Japan)

cast
Kanbei Shimada Takashi Shimura
Kikuchiyo Toshirô Mifune
Gorobei Katayama Yoshio Inaba
Kyuzo Seiji Miyaguchi
Heihachi Hayashida
Minoru Chiaki
Shichiroji Daisuke Katô
Katsushiro Isao Kimura
Manzo, father of Shino
Kamatari Fujiwara
Shino Keiko Tsushima
Yohei Bokuzen Hidari
Mosuke Yoshio Kosugi
Rikichi Yoshio Tsuchiya
Gisaku, the Old Man
Kokuten Kodo
Bandit Leader Kichijiro Ueda